American History Stories

101 True and Fascinating Tales of Major Events and People from the United States' Past

Table of Contents

Introduction

Step into the captivating tapestry of American history, a sweeping chronicle that weaves triumphs, tribulations, moments of explosive change, and quiet courage. From the rugged beginnings in the colonial era to the dawn of a new nation to the unrelenting march toward progress, each chapter in this extraordinary narrative unveils pivotal events that have shaped the United States as we know it today. Delve into riveting tales of exploration, wars that reshaped continents, social movements that challenged the status quo, and groundbreaking advancements that propelled the nation into the modern age.

Get ready for a captivating journey through time as we uncover an intriguing collection of facts, interesting stories, and fascinating characters in the realm of American history.

Section 1 – From the Mystery of Roanoke to a New Nation: Journey through Early American History

In the late 16th and early 17th centuries, America witnessed significant historical events that laid the foundation for its future. From the mysterious disappearance of the Roanoke Colony to the establishment of Jamestown in Virginia, these important moments shaped American history.

These fascinating tales about the Thirteen Colonies will shed new light on a part of American history that tends to get written off as dull. Discover why these formative events set a course for America's path to becoming an independent nation.

1. Roanoke Colony was founded in 1585. It was the first English settlement in North America, but this colony off the coast of North Carolina was short-lived. The people living there mysteriously disappeared when the next ship arrived five years later.

    Led by Governor John White, the colony aimed to become the first permanent English settlement in the New World. White realized the colonists could not survive without additional supplies. In 1587, White returned to England. The trip was hard on his crew, and several men died on the voyage. Once they returned to England, they encountered more problems. England and Spain were at war with each other. White would not be returning to Roanoke anytime soon.

When White returned to Roanoke in 1590, he found the colony completely abandoned. The only clues to their fate were the words "CROATOAN" carved into a tree and "CRO" etched into the fort's gatepost.

What happened to the colony is a mystery to this day. The fate of the Roanoke colonists captivates historians and has fueled speculation for centuries.

Some suggest the colonists relocated to Croatoan Island (present-day Hatteras Island). This hypothesis is supported by the inscriptions left in Roanoke and the existence of a tribe known as the Croatans who inhabited the island at the time. Others propose that the colonists merged with local Native American tribes, assimilating into their cultures and abandoning their English identity. Others believe the colonists were wiped out by Native American attacks. And some of the more far-fetched theories include aliens!

Besides this enduring mystery, the Roanoke Colony is remarkable for another reason. Virginia Dare was born in Roanoke in 1587, the first English-born child. She was the granddaughter of John White. Of course, nothing is known about her life since the colonists mysteriously vanished, but many places in the US, especially in North Carolina, have been named after her.

2. Did you know the early colonists of Jamestown had to resort to cannibalism to stay alive?

Jamestown was established in 1607 and became North America's first permanent English settlement. Jamestown was founded in present-day Virginia by the Virginia Company of London, a joint-stock company seeking economic opportunities and a foothold in the New World.

When the colonists arrived in Jamestown, it was too late in the year to plant crops. The region was also seeing one of the worst droughts in its history. It was so severe that it even impacted the local Powhatan tribe. Nevertheless, they made an attempt to eke out an existence. The next year, supply ships arrived with aid and more hungry mouths to feed.

At the beginning of the long winter in 1609, around five hundred settlers were in Jamestown. By the time winter was over, there would only be sixty-one left. What happened? Well, there just was not enough food for all the people. The plan had been to trade food with the Native Americans, so they had grown a small number of crops. Although they made friendly contact with the Native Americans, that ended when John Smith was sent back to England after being injured in a gunpowder accident.

People ate cats, dogs, rats –and even each other – to survive the winter. George Percy, a colonist in Jamestown, stated, "The living dug up and ate corpses, and that a husband killed his wife and then butchered her, preserved her with salt, and ate parts of her before he was caught." Archaeological evidence confirms that cannibalism did indeed take place during what is now known as the Starving Time.

Although that winter was incredibly tough and decimated the colony's population, more people arrived in 1610. Once tobacco began to be exported in 1612, more people flocked to the colony to get it on this profitable venture. Jamestown was the cornerstone of British colonization and was pivotal in shaping American history.

3. The first enslaved Africans were brought to Virginia in August 1619. A Dutch ship brought about twenty enslaved people to Jamestown, becoming one of the earliest instances of forced labor and slavery within what would become the United States. Slavery would become deeply entrenched in the South's economy, shaping its agricultural practices, social dynamics, and political landscape.

The Middle Passage was the second leg of the transatlantic slave trade. Africans were forcibly taken from their homes and transported to the Americas. Their journey was characterized by unimaginable cruelty and suffering. Cramped into the holds of slave ships, Africans were subjected to horrendous conditions. They were often chained together, malnourished, and denied basic sanitation. The journey was fraught with disease, overcrowding, and psychological torment, with many perishing before reaching their destination. At least two million Africans died while traveling the Middle Passage.

The brutal reality of the transatlantic slave trade is vividly portrayed in the 1997 historical drama *Amistad*, directed by Steven Spielberg. The film tells the true story of a group of enslaved Africans who mutinied aboard the slave ship *Amistad* and eventually found themselves in a legal battle for their freedom. They won, which helped propel the abolitionist movement.

The 1977 television miniseries *Roots*, based on Alex Haley's novel, provides a broader and more comprehensive look at the experience of slavery. The miniseries follows the life of Kunta Kinte, a young Mandinka man from West Africa who is captured and sold into slavery in the United States. *Roots* depicts the harsh realities of plantation life, including the brutal labor slaves were forced to endure, the separation of families, and the constant threat of violence. It also explores the resilience and strength of the enslaved community, their unbroken spirit, and their determination to maintain their cultural identity.

4. In 1620, a group known as the Pilgrims sought religious freedom and settled at Plymouth Rock after their journey aboard the *Mayflower*. While still on board the ship, they signed an agreement for self-governance called the Mayflower Compact. The Mayflower Compact marked a turning point in American history, establishing a foundation for self-rule and democratic ideals that would shape the nation's development.

However, the initial years for the Pilgrims were anything but smooth sailing. A brutal winter decimated their ranks, leaving them weak and on the brink of starvation. Squanto, a Patuxet man fluent in English who had been kidnapped and returned to his tribe years before, became a vital link, teaching the Pilgrims how to fish, farm, and navigate the unforgiving landscape.

After a grueling harvest season, Governor William Bradford proposed a three-day feast to express gratitude for their newfound survival and to forge a stronger bond with their Wampanoag allies. Chief Massasoit and his people joined the festivities, bringing deer, pumpkins, and dried berries to share alongside the Pilgrims' wild turkey, clams, and homemade sassafras ale. Laughter and shared stories filled the air as games were played and songs sung in both familiar and unfamiliar tongues.

This wasn't just a celebratory feast; it was a strategic move. The shared meal symbolized a fragile peace treaty built on mutual dependence and cautious friendship. While future years would witness conflict and tension, this moment at Plymouth offered a flickering hope for coexistence between two cultures that had collided on foreign shores.

This spirit of shared gratitude and unity resonated with President Abraham Lincoln during the Civil War, leading him to declare the first national Thanksgiving in 1863. Almost two hundred years later, in 1942, President Franklin D. Roosevelt moved Thanksgiving from the last Thursday in November to the fourth Thursday, a change that remains in effect today. These proclamations reflected the evolving significance of Thanksgiving from a local harvest celebration to a national holiday that symbolized unity, gratitude, and the shared values that bind Americans together.

The First Thanksgiving at Plymouth by Jennie A. Brownscombe (1914).
https://commons.wikimedia.org/wiki/File:Thanksgiving-Brownscombe.jpg

5. In 1630, Puritans led by John Winthrop settled in a new colony called the Massachusetts Bay Colony, with Boston as its center. They aimed to create a "city on a hill," a sort of "guiding light."

The colony did indeed become influential during the early colonial era.

Under Winthrop's leadership, the Puritans established a strict social and religious order based on their interpretation of the Bible. They believed they were chosen by God to create a "New England" that would be a shining example of Christian virtue.

Despite the Puritans leaving England to be able to worship as they pleased, they were not very tolerant of others. As more people arrived, some people disagreed with their beliefs and practices. The Puritans were not happy with this turn of events. One of the most well-known examples is the Puritan attitude and actions toward the Religious Society of Friends, more commonly known as the Quakers.

The arrival of the Quakers in Massachusetts in the 1650s was met with hostility from the Puritan authorities. The Quakers' beliefs, which diverged from the strict Puritan orthodoxy, were seen as a threat to the established order. The Quakers' pacifism, rejection of formal clergy, and emphasis on inner experience were all considered dangerous and subversive.

In response, the Massachusetts Bay Colony passed a series of laws against the Quakers, prohibiting them from entering the colony, attending Quaker meetings, or publishing Quaker literature. Quakers who violated these laws were subject to fines, whippings, and even banishment.

The most severe punishment was reserved for those who entered the colony but did not actually live there. In 1659, four Quakers – Mary Dyer, Marmaduke Stephenson, William Robinson, and William Leddra – were executed by hanging for returning to Massachusetts after being banished. Their deaths marked the climax of Quaker persecution in Massachusetts.

The Toleration Act of 1689 (passed by the English Parliament) brought an end to the persecution of Quakers in Massachusetts. The act granted toleration to all Protestants, including Quakers, and prohibited the Massachusetts government from passing laws that interfered with religious freedom.

6. You may have noticed that Catholics were not listed when discussing the Toleration Act. The Reformation changed many

things in England, including the state religion. In 1632, Maryland was founded as a haven for Catholics, who were being persecuted in England.

Cecil Calvert – otherwise known as Lord Baltimore – established Maryland as a proprietary colony to create a safe space for Catholics to practice their religion freely. While the Puritans are often cited as pioneers for religious freedom, Plymouth Colony and the Massachusetts Bay Colony were not tolerant of Catholics.

In 1649, the Maryland General Assembly passed the Maryland Toleration Act, which granted religious freedom to all Christians who believed in the Trinity. This was a groundbreaking piece of legislation at the time, as most other colonies in what would become the United States were dominated by Puritans, most of whom were hostile to Catholicism.

The Maryland Toleration Act was not without its limitations. It only applied to Christians and did not guarantee equal rights for all religious groups. However, it was a significant step forward in terms of religious tolerance in the New World.

Many people believe that Maryland, being founded as a safe place for Catholics, was named for the Virgin Mary or even Queen Mary I, but it was not. It was named after the wife of King Charles I, Henrietta Maria, the daughter of King Henry IV of France and Queen Marie de' Medici. Henry IV was well acquainted with religious strife in his own country, having converted to Catholicism to become king during a time of extreme religious tension.

7. As the years passed, conflict arose between European settlers and Native American tribes over land disputes, competition for resources and trade, and cultural differences. The Pequot War was one of them. This war had profound implications for relations between colonizers and indigenous people in New England.

On one side were the English colonists, represented by Massachusetts Bay Colony, Plymouth Colony, and Saybrook Colony (an English colony in Connecticut). Led by figures like John Mason and John Endecott, these colonists sought to expand their territory and assert their dominance over the region.

On the other side stood the Pequots, a powerful Native American tribe controlling a vast territory in present-day southeastern Connecticut. Led by sachems (tribal leaders) Sassacus and Wequashcuk – one of the earliest Native American converts to Christianity – the Pequots sought to protect their ancestral lands and resist the expanding colonial presence.

The war began in earnest in 1636 when the Pequots attacked a group of English settlers near Mystic, Connecticut. In response, the colonists launched a series of brutal attacks on Pequot villages, culminating in the infamous Mystic massacre.

The Pequot village, located on Mystic River, only had two exits. The English and their Native American allies, who were upset with the Pequots' actions, blocked the exits and set fire to the village. The only Pequot survivors were the warriors who escaped the burning village. This event, in which hundreds of Pequot men, women, and children were killed, marked a turning point in the war.

By the end of 1637, the Pequots had been largely defeated. Their tribe was decimated. Estimates suggest that around seven hundred Pequots had been killed, while the English suffered around seventy casualties. Hundreds of Pequots were sold into slavery, and some Pequots were given to tribes that had allied with the English.

The war had a profound impact on the relations between the English colonists and the Native American tribes of New England, setting the stage for further conflict and displacement in the region.

This war also demonstrates what happened to many Native American tribes. However, unlike some tribes, the Pequots are still around today. Much of their culture, including their language, had been supplanted by English. Today, the Pequot are making efforts to preserve their culture, including analyzing documents to find clues to their language.

8. King Philip's War, also known as Metacomet's War, the First Indian War, or the Great Narragansett War, was the deadliest conflict between Europeans and Native Americans during the colonial era. It erupted in 1675 when Metacomet, the

Wampanoag sachem, created a broad alliance of Native American tribes to resist the expansionist policies of the English colonists in New England. Metacomet was known as King Philip by the English.

The war's roots lay in the deep-seated resentment among Native Americans toward the encroachment of English settlers on their ancestral lands. The English settlements disrupted their traditional hunting and fishing grounds, and the imposition of religious and cultural practices clashed with their own.

The war raged for over a year, from 1675 to 1676, and left a trail of death and destruction on both sides. Despite their superior firepower and numbers, the English colonists struggled to subdue the Native American resistance.

The turning point came in December 1675 when the English launched a surprise attack on the Narragansetts' fortified stronghold in the Great Swamp Fight. The settlement's moat had frozen in the cold December weather. The English were able to cross over the moat easily and set fire to the settlement.

Many consider the attack a massacre, with hundreds of Native Americans killed, including many women and children. Many Native Americans ran into the frozen swampland, where hundreds died from their wounds and the cold.

This devastating blow crippled the Native American alliance, and the war gradually turned in favor of the English. By the spring of 1676, most Native American resistance had been crushed.

King Philip's War was one of the deadliest conflicts in American history, with an estimated 3,000 to 6,000 Native Americans and over 2,000 English colonists killed. The war also resulted in the displacement of many Native American tribes and the destruction of their villages and communities.

An illustration of the Great Swamp Fight.

9. The Elizabeth Key Case was a landmark legal proceeding that took place in the Virginia Colony in the mid-17th century. It had significant implications for the legal status of enslaved individuals and the development of racialized slavery in colonial America.

Elizabeth Key, also known as Elizabeth Key Grinstead, was born in the Virginia Colony in the 1630s to an Englishman named Thomas Key and an enslaved African woman named Joan. Initially, she was considered an indentured servant. However, her status changed after her father's death. His heirs said that Key was a slave and that she belonged to the estate.

In 1655, Elizabeth Key filed a lawsuit for her freedom. She argued that she should not be enslaved because her father was an Englishman and a free man and because she had been baptized as a Christian. Her case raised complex legal and moral questions about the status of mixed-race individuals and the impact of Christian baptism on enslavement.

In 1656, the Virginia court ruled in favor of Elizabeth Key, declaring that she should be set free. The court recognized the principle of English common law, which did not recognize perpetual servitude. Under English law, the status of a child typically followed that of the father. Since Elizabeth's father was a free Englishman, the court determined that she could not be held in perpetual servitude.

Elizabeth's baptism as a Christian was also considered a factor in her favor. Some legal and moral arguments at the time suggested that Christians should not be held in slavery.

The Elizabeth Key Case set an important legal precedent in the Virginia Colony. It established that the status of children born to enslaved mothers could be influenced by the status of their fathers, especially if their fathers were free Englishmen. This distinction between the children of English fathers and African mothers contributed to the gradual development of a racialized system of slavery in colonial America.

10. Some of the most interesting stories in history involve pirates. Would you be shocked to know that pirates were a part of colonial American history?

Edward Teach, commonly known as Blackbeard, was one of the most feared and notorious pirates of the early 18th century. By 1718, he had established a stronghold in the coastal waters of the American colonies, particularly around the Outer Banks and the entrance to Pamlico Sound. Blackbeard's fleet included the *Queen Anne's Revenge*, a former French slave ship he had captured and heavily armed.

The British colonial authorities, led by Lieutenant Governor Alexander Spotswood of Virginia, were determined to put an end to Blackbeard's piracy. Spotswood organized a naval expedition to capture or kill Blackbeard and his crew. He appointed Lieutenant Robert Maynard to lead this mission.

Maynard and his men located Blackbeard's ships anchored at Ocracoke Inlet. On the morning of November 22nd, 1718, the two sides engaged in a fierce battle. Blackbeard and his crew put up a determined defense, and the fight was brutal and intense. During the battle, Blackbeard was shot multiple times and sustained numerous wounds. Ultimately, Blackbeard was finally killed, and his ship, the *Queen Anne's Revenge*, was captured. Maynard's forces took several of Blackbeard's crew members prisoner, while others were killed in the battle or escaped into the nearby swamps.

Blackbeard's death marked a significant victory for the colonial authorities in their efforts to combat piracy in the Atlantic coastal waters. His severed head was later displayed on the bow of Maynard's ship as evidence of his demise. This event had a lasting impact on the perception of piracy and the authority of colonial governments in the New World. Blackbeard's legend and the story of his last battle continue to capture people's imaginations to this day!

Section 2 – From Wars to Freedom: A Journey through American History from 1754 to 1791

Join us on an exciting adventure through early American history! Discover the important events that shaped the United States, from battles fought in the French and Indian War to the heroic struggles for independence in the Revolutionary War. Witness how a new nation was born with a constitution built on freedom.

11. George Washington was a veteran of more than just the American Revolution. He also fought in the French and Indian War between 1754 and 1763. Although the French and Indian War is considered a theater of the Seven Years' War, it actually began before that war erupted in continental Europe

Tensions arose between the British and the French over land in the Ohio Valley. The British Ohio Company of Virginia was granted the land, but the French began to move in. The Virginians were worried that the French would stake a claim. They sent twenty-one-year-old George Washington to tell the French to leave.

Washington delivered the message, but the French refused to leave. He was granted the commission of lieutenant colonel and sent back to the frontier with a company of men.

Meanwhile, the French sent Joseph Coulon de Villiers de Jumonville with a small unit of men to warn Washington to leave the area. Washington and Tanacharison, the leader of the Mingo people, discovered the French camp and decided to attack it.

It is not known what exactly happened in the Battle of Jumonville Glen. The few things that are known are that the battle only lasted around fifteen minutes and that most of the French were either killed or taken prisoner. Jumonville was killed in the action. Several accounts say that Tanacharison killed Jumonville, crushing his skull with a tomahawk.

Washington moved his men to Fort Necessity, where they were attacked by the French. Washington eventually surrendered, which marked the only time he ever surrendered a battle. In the document he was forced to sign, Washington admitted that Jumonville and his men had been assassinated. Jumonville was sent to warn the British to leave, not actually war with them. However, Washington did not know how to read French, and his translator did a poor job explaining what was in the document. Nevertheless, the stage was set for a war.

The French and Indian War also highlighted the increased involvement of Native American tribes in colonial affairs. Various tribes, including the Iroquois Confederacy and the Algonquin Confederacy, aligned themselves with either the British or the French. The tribes were often driven by historical relationships, trade interests, and religious beliefs. These alliances added another layer of complexity to the war, influencing its course and demonstrating the intricate dynamics between European powers and Native American nations.

France would go on to lose the war, which allowed the British to expand their territory in North America. The war would also prove to be troublesome on the economic front for Britain, which was forced to raise taxes on the American colonists. These taxes were not received well, and cries for independence would eventually echo throughout the Thirteen Colonies.

12. On March 5th, 1770, the Boston Massacre occurred. British soldiers killed five colonists during a confrontation in Boston; one of the victims, Crispus Attucks, was an African American

sailor who became an unwitting symbol of the growing unrest.

On the evening of the incident, a crowd of colonists gathered near the Custom House, where British soldiers stood guard. Several colonists began taunting them and throwing items like stones and snowballs. One soldier eventually fired his weapon, which caused other soldiers to fire theirs. Three people died then; two others later died of their wounds. It is believed Crispus Attucks was the first person to be killed in the massacre. Some consider him the first casualty of the American Revolution.

While the massacre is an interesting story in and of itself, let's take a look at the aftermath of the massacre. John Adams, a young lawyer and an outspoken critic of British policies, found himself defending the British soldiers. Despite the public outcry and the overwhelming evidence against the soldiers, Adams believed these men demanded a fair trial.

Adams argued passionately for the soldiers' right to legal representation, stating that "every person charged with a crime must have the benefit of counsel." Though unpopular at the time, Adams's defense of the British soldiers earned him the respect of both sides and established him as a brilliant legal mind and a champion of justice. His actions during the trial solidified his reputation as a defender of the rights of the accused, a legacy that would continue to resonate throughout his political career.

Of the eight soldiers charged with murder, six were acquitted. Two were convicted of manslaughter and branded on their hands. This outcome, though controversial, demonstrated that even in a time of heightened tensions, the principles of fair justice could prevail. Adams would later sign the Declaration of Independence and become the second president of the United States.

13. The Boston Tea Party was a protest against the British Tea Act of 1773, which granted the British East India Company a monopoly on tea sales in the American colonies and imposed a tax on tea. In an act of defiance against "taxation without representation," the Patriots boarded British tea ships and threw the tea into Boston Harbor. Over three hundred chests of tea were thrown into the water, with the losses amounting to almost two million dollars today.

Most people are familiar with the Boston Tea Party. It was a famous event in American history that played a pivotal role in the lead-up to the American Revolution. However, many people may be unfamiliar with a woman named Sarah Bradlee Fulton.

Sarah Bradlee Fulton was the wife of John Fulton, a member of the Sons of Liberty, a secret organization that played a key role in the protest against British taxation and policies in the American colonies. On the night of December 16th, 1773, when the Boston Tea Party took place, Sarah Bradlee Fulton supported the cause by assisting the Patriots in their protest against the British Tea Act. It is believed Sarah came up with the idea of having the protesters disguise themselves as Mohawks. Sarah and other women helped prepare for the event by making the disguises for the men. They sewed these disguises using blankets and feathers. They also helped paint the men's faces. This brilliant idea ensured that the Patriots could carry out their act of defiance without being easily recognized.

Sarah Bradlee Fulton's involvement in supporting the protest by creating disguises for the participants highlights the significant contributions of women to the American Revolution and the cause of colonial independence. Their roles extended beyond traditional domestic spheres and played a crucial part in the events leading up to the American Revolution.

A lithograph of the Boston Tea Party.
https://commons.wikimedia.org/wiki/File:Boston_Tea_Party_Currier_colored.jpg

14. On April 19th, 1775, fighting erupted at Lexington and Concord in Massachusetts, marking the start of armed conflict between American militiamen, called Minutemen, and British troops. Famed writer Ralph Waldo Emerson would later describe the fighting. He called the opening shots of the battle "the shot heard 'round the world." The phrase is meant to convey the idea that these shots were not just some random skirmish but rather a momentous event that would have far-reaching consequences.

The Battles of Lexington and Concord were not mere skirmishes; they were the opening salvos of the American Revolutionary War. Under General Thomas Gage's command, the British sought to seize military supplies from the colonists in Concord. However, they were met with fierce resistance from the Minutemen, a group of armed colonists prepared to fight for their independence.

The fighting at Lexington and Concord was intense and bloody. The British suffered heavy casualties, with 73 soldiers killed and 174 wounded. Though outnumbered and outgunned, the colonists fought valiantly, suffering forty-nine deaths and thirty-nine wounded.

To this day, no one is quite sure who took that "shot heard 'round the world." The British told the American militias to disband. John Parker, the captain of the militia, told his men to go home. However, there was so much confusion, with people yelling at each other, that some men didn't leave or left very slowly. Eventually, a shot rang out, and the rest was history.

These battles dealt a significant blow to British morale. The British underestimated the colonists' resolve, expecting to quell the uprising quickly. However, the Minutemen's resistance demonstrated that the colonists would not be easily subdued, shaking British confidence.

The Battles of Lexington and Concord stand as a testament to the courage and determination of the American colonists in their fight for independence. They were not just military engagements; they were the opening chapter in the struggle for a new nation.

15. On July 4th, 1776, the Second Continental Congress adopted the Declaration of Independence, a document that had been drafted by Thomas Jefferson and had been altered slightly by Benjamin

Franklin and John Adams. As you may have guessed, the Declaration of Independence formally proclaimed the colonies' independence from Great Britain.

The Declaration of Independence outlined the grievances of the American colonists against the British Crown, including taxation without representation, the quartering of British troops in the colonies, and the denial of trial by jury. About a quarter of the fifty-six signers of the Declaration of Independence were imprisoned, exiled, or otherwise persecuted by the British during the Revolutionary War. Three signers lost their lives during or because of the war.

Thomas Jefferson was the man most responsible for the content and actual writing of the Declaration of Independence. Jefferson was the poet/philosopher of the American Revolution. His eloquent pen penned the immortal lines of the Declaration of Independence, forever etching the ideals of liberty and equality into the American consciousness.

However, Jefferson wasn't just a wordsmith. He was a complex figure. He was a slave owner who grappled with the contradictions of his own beliefs. Even though he was a passionate advocate for democracy, he also harbored aristocratic tendencies. He and John Adams, who were at times political rivals, were also fast friends later in life, and their letters to each other provide important insights into the founding of America and its political ideas. Both men died on the same day – July 4th, 1826 – fifty years to the day after the new nation was announced with the Declaration of Independence!

Jefferson's official presidential portrait.

16. Perhaps the most famous battle of the Revolutionary War was the Battle of Trenton. The battle resulted in an astounding American victory, but it is also famous because of the painting *Washington Crossing the Delaware*, which was actually painted seventy-five years later by a German painter who had never been to America.

Under a biting December wind, General George Washington undertook a daring gamble on the banks of the Delaware. The Continental Army, dwindling and demoralized, faced winter's unforgiving grip and whispers of disbandment. Yet, on Christmas night, 1776, Washington led a ragged force across the icy river, aiming for a surprise attack on Hessian troops garrisoned in Trenton.

The plan was audacious. Crossing in treacherous conditions, the American column marched ten miles through the frigid night, arriving at Trenton before dawn. Hessian forces, lulled by Christmas festivities, were caught unprepared. The assault, led by Washington himself, proved swift and decisive. The Hessian ranks crumbled under the surprise American assault, and their commander fell in the opening volleys. Nearly two-thirds of the Hessian force surrendered within an hour, delivering a much-needed victory for the beleaguered colonists.

The Battle of Trenton was a strategic masterpiece. It rekindled hope within the Continental Army, stemming the tide of desertion. Washington's decisive leadership and the army's unexpected success shattered the British aura of invincibility, bolstering morale and demonstrating American resilience. Though a small engagement, the Battle of Trenton reverberated across the colonies, proving the nascent nation's ability to strike back and reigniting the flames of revolution.

17. In September 1781, the tide of the American Revolution culminated in the pivotal Battle of Yorktown in Virginia. Trapped on a peninsula and cut off by relentless Franco-American forces under General Washington and General Rochambeau, British General Lord Cornwallis faced a dire predicament.

The siege itself was a meticulous orchestration of firepower and strategy. American and French engineers constructed a ring of fortifications that steadily constricted the British defensive perimeter. Heavy cannons pounded the British positions relentlessly, while French naval superiority ensured no escape route by sea. Facing imminent assault and lacking reinforcements, Cornwallis attempted a desperate breakout, only to be repelled. On October 19th, with dwindling supplies and mounting casualties, he surrendered his entire army, effectively ending major land operations in the American Revolution.

Adding another layer of intrigue to this pivotal moment is the story of "The World Turned Upside Down." According to historical accounts, the British band, as customary, played a march to honor the victors after the formal surrender. However, instead of a traditional British tune, they surprisingly struck up the melody of "The World Turned Upside Down," a ballad often associated with English social unrest and upheaval.

While the exact motivation behind this choice remains shrouded in speculation, it resonated with the gravity of the situation. For the newly formed American nation, it mirrored the realization of their revolutionary goals; the colonists' world, formerly dominated by British rule, had indeed turned upside down. For the defeated British, it was a bittersweet acknowledgment of their altered fortunes.

On September 3rd, 1783, the Treaty of Paris was signed, and the Revolutionary War was brought to a close. The treaty formally recognized the United States as an independent nation. This momentous agreement marked a turning point in world history, establishing a new balance of power and ushering in the era of American democracy.

18. On September 17th, 1787, the Constitutional Convention in Philadelphia concluded with delegates signing the United States Constitution, a landmark document that established the framework for a new federal government. The Constitution, with its system of checks and balances, separation of powers, and emphasis on individual rights, stands as a cornerstone of American democracy and a testament to the power of collective wisdom.

While the American Constitution is a unique document, many of its ideas came to the Founding Fathers through English constitutional history and the Enlightenment thinkers of France and Great Britain in the early 1700s. However, some historians contend the Constitution was inspired by another group of people: the Native American Iroquois Confederation in the border areas of the United States and Canada.

It must be emphasized that the Iroquois Confederacy's direct influence on the Articles of Confederation and the Constitution is debated among historians. However, it is possible that their political structure offered an intriguing model for the nascent American government.

The Iroquois Confederacy comprised six independent nations united by a common council, the *Grand Council*. They practiced a form of confederation that balanced individual tribal autonomy with collective decision-making. This might have resonated with the American colonists, who sought unity against British rule while cherishing their own sovereignty. The Articles of Confederation, the first governing document of the United States, reflected this influence, creating a weak central government reliant on unanimous consent from independent states.

However, the Iroquois Confederacy's inherent limitations became evident. As individual Iroquois nations prioritized their needs, unified action often faltered, ultimately contributing to their vulnerability against European encroachment. This served as a cautionary tale for the American framers. When drafting the Constitution, they sought to strengthen the central government while still honoring state autonomy. The bicameral Congress, with its House of Representatives reflecting individual states and the Senate representing equal representation for all, mirrored the Iroquois approach to balancing local and national interests.

19. On April 30th, 1789, George Washington was elected as the first president of the United States. Washington's presidency, from 1789 to 1797, was paramount in shaping the early United States. His leadership during this critical formative period established precedents for the presidency, fostered national unity, and laid the foundation for a strong and stable government.

Many stories and legends have sprung up about George Washington. Let's go over three of the most popular.

The Cherry Tree: The image of young George chopping down a cherry tree and confessing his deed to his stern father, declaring, "I cannot tell a lie," is ingrained in American legend. However, the story, first published in Parson Mason Weems's 1806 biography, likely originated as a morality tale aimed at children rather than a historical account. While Washington was undoubtedly known for his integrity, the cherry tree myth, with its idealized portrayal, paints an unrealistic picture of Washington's life and downplays the complex motivations governing his actions.

Wooden Teeth: Perhaps one of the most enduring and bizarre myths revolves around Washington's teeth. Images often depict him with wooden dentures. While Washington suffered from severe dental problems throughout his life and experimented with various dentures made from diverse materials, including hippopotamus ivory and human teeth, there's no evidence he ever utilized wooden ones. This myth likely arose from misinterpretations of historical descriptions and was fueled by caricatures depicting him with an exaggerated, wooden grin.

Throwing a Silver Dollar across the Potomac: For many years, American grade-school students were taught a story about Washington throwing a coin across the wide Potomac River. It's a captivating image, but it is false. The truth, like many historical narratives, is nuanced. While there's mention of Washington hurling an object (not a silver dollar) as a teen across the Rappahannock, not the much wider Potomac, primary sources remain elusive. The iconic silver dollar and majestic river are later embellishments, making Washington a larger-than-life legend.

This myth, though factually shaky, served a purpose. It cemented perceptions of Washington as an exceptional figure, capable of extraordinary feats even before his presidential ascent. But it's a reminder to critically examine historical narratives and separate romanticized portrayals from documented facts.

20. John Leland was a prominent Baptist preacher in Virginia during the late 18th century. He fervently advocated for religious liberty and separation of church and state. At the time, Virginia had an established state church, the Anglican Church (Church of England), which received government support and privileges. Leland, as a Baptist, experienced religious discrimination and believed in the importance of protecting religious freedom for all.

During the debate over the ratification of the US Constitution, Leland was initially skeptical of the document because it lacked explicit protections for individual rights, including religious freedom. He was concerned that without such protections, the federal government might interfere with religious practices and beliefs.

James Madison, a key figure in drafting the Constitution, was running for a seat in the first US Congress. Leland, along with other Baptists and religious minorities, sought assurances from Madison that he would support amendments to the Constitution that would protect individual liberties. In 1788, Leland met with Madison in Orange County, Virginia, and presented him with a list of proposed amendments, including those focused on religious freedom. Madison listened to Leland's concerns and promised to support amendments safeguarding these rights.

When Madison was elected to the first Congress, he followed through on his promise by introducing a series of amendments to the Constitution, which would later become the Bill of Rights. Among these amendments was the First Amendment, which includes the Establishment Clause and the Free Exercise Clause, guaranteeing religious freedom and prohibiting the establishment of a state religion.

John Leland's advocacy for religious freedom and his meeting with James Madison played a significant role in shaping the inclusion of religious liberty protections in the Bill of Rights. His dedication to the principle of religious freedom helped ensure that it became a fundamental part of the US Constitution, protecting the rights of all citizens to practice their religion freely.

Section 3 – The Expansion of America and the Reform Era

Next, we will explore the fascinating period of expansion and reform in US history. Discover how America grew both geographically and socially through westward expansion, the Trail of Tears, and the women's suffrage movement. This was a pivotal time in US history; *these fascinating stories will show why.*

21. In 1803, President Thomas Jefferson commissioned Meriwether Lewis and William Clark to lead an expedition into the newly acquired Louisiana Territory. Their primary mission was to explore and map the western part of the continent and seek a water route to the Pacific Ocean. At the time, there was a belief that the Northwest Passage might exist – a passage that would greatly facilitate trade and transportation.

    During their journey westward, Lewis and Clark's expedition encountered numerous challenges, including harsh weather, difficult terrain, and encounters with Native American tribes. However, one of the most memorable incidents occurred when they encountered a grizzly bear in what is now North Dakota in 1805.

    On May 14th, 1805, Meriwether Lewis was hunting alone when he encountered a massive grizzly bear. The bear charged at Lewis, who was armed only with a small caliber weapon. Lewis shot the bear, but it didn't stop. He fired several more shots, and eventually, the bear fell only feet away from him.

Lewis and his men estimated the bear's weight at over six hundred pounds. It was a massive grizzly, and its size and aggression were unlike anything they had encountered before. The encounter with the grizzly bear highlighted the dangers and challenges faced by the expedition as they ventured into uncharted territory. It also illustrated the need for keen marksmanship and resourcefulness in surviving the wilderness.

Despite the hardships and dangers, Lewis and Clark's expedition was a remarkable success. They mapped vast stretches of land, made contact with indigenous peoples, documented new plant and animal species, and disproved the existence of a continuous US water route to the Pacific. Their journey helped expand America's understanding of the western part of the continent and paved the way for future westward expansion.

22. The War of 1812 erupted amid trade disputes and British interference in American shipping. Britain, which was embroiled in its own struggle in the Napoleonic Wars, saw the young American republic as a thorn in its side, as America was a competitor on the seas and a haven for British deserters. The tipping point came when the British Royal Navy seized American ships and impressed sailors into their service, a blatant affront to American sovereignty.

Did you know that future President Andrew Jackson fought in the War of 1812? Or that his most famous moment in the war occurred after the war had ended?

At the time of the Battle of New Orleans, Major General Andrew Jackson was in command of American forces in the city. Jackson's forces consisted of a diverse mix of regular soldiers, local militia, free African Americans, and even pirates, such as Jean Lafitte and his privateers. The British, led by General Edward Pakenham, launched a major assault on the American position on January 8th, 1815.

Despite being outnumbered, Jackson's troops, fortified behind earthworks, inflicted heavy casualties on the British. The British suffered over two thousand casualties, including the death of General Pakenham, while the American forces sustained only a few dozen casualties. The Battle of New Orleans was a resounding American victory and is often regarded as one of the most decisive battles of the War of 1812.

What makes this battle particularly interesting is that it was fought after the Treaty of Ghent had been signed on December 24th, 1814, in Belgium, officially ending the war. However, due to the slow pace of communications in the early 19th century, news of the treaty's ratification did not reach the United States until after the battle had been fought.

The Battle of New Orleans bolstered American morale and national pride, as it was seen as a significant victory over a well-trained British force. It also had political implications, as Andrew Jackson's success in defending New Orleans contributed to his rise as a national hero and eventually played a role in his successful presidential campaign in 1828.

Painting of the Battle of New Orleans by Jean Hyacinthe de Laclotte.
https://commons.wikimedia.org/wiki/File:Battle_of_New_Orleans,_Jean_Hyacinthe_de_Laclotte.jpg

23. In the early 1830s, tensions were rising between American settlers and Mexican authorities in the Mexican province of Texas. The Mexican government, under President Antonio

López de Santa Anna, began to assert greater control over Texas, leading to discontent among the American settlers.

In 1831, the Mexican government provided a small cannon to the settlement of Gonzales for defense against local Native American tribes. The cannon was small, often referred to as a "six-pounder," and it had limited military significance. In September 1835, as tensions between Texans and Mexican authorities grew, a detachment of Mexican soldiers was sent to Gonzales to retrieve the cannon. They demanded its return, fearing that it could be used against Mexican forces in a potential uprising.

The Texans in Gonzales, led by George W. Collingsworth and supported by other settlers, responded defiantly to the Mexican demand. They refused to return the cannon and instead raised a homemade flag featuring a black cannon, a star, and the words "Come and Take It."

This flag and the Texan response essentially became a declaration of defiance. The Mexican detachment and the Texans exchanged shots on October 2nd, 1835, marking the beginning of the Texas Revolution. The Battle of Gonzales was a small skirmish but had profound symbolic significance.

Despite the limited military importance of the cannon, the Texans managed to drive off the Mexican forces. They retained the cannon as a symbol of their determination to resist Mexican authority. The phrase "Come and Take It" became a rallying cry for Texian forces throughout the Texas Revolution. It symbolized their resolve to fight for their independence and resist Mexican control.

The "Come and Take It" flag and the cannon remain enduring symbols of Texan pride and resistance to oppression. The cannon is preserved and displayed at the Gonzales Memorial Museum, and the flag's imagery is still associated with the spirit of Texan independence.

24. The Indian Removal Act was signed into law by President Andrew Jackson in 1830. The act led to the forced relocation of thousands of Cherokee, Creek, Seminole, and other indigenous tribes from their ancestral lands. Mainstream historians believe anywhere between four and ten thousand people died or were

killed on the Trail of Tears.

Cherokee leader John Ross played a prominent role in resisting the forced removal of the Cherokee Nation. John Ross, born in 1790, was of mixed Cherokee and Scottish ancestry. He became a leader within the Cherokee Nation and served as the principal chief from 1828 to 1866.

As the president of the Cherokee Nation, Ross worked tirelessly to use legal means to resist removal. The Cherokee people established a written constitution modeled after that of the United States in 1827. The following year, Georgia determined that the constitution was invalid and that the Cherokee were subject to Georgia laws.

John Ross brought the landmark case *Cherokee Nation v. Georgia* (1831) to the Supreme Court. The court ruled that it had no jurisdiction to listen to the case. In *Worcester v. Georgia* (1832), the court ruled that the state of Georgia had no authority over Cherokee lands, declaring the Cherokee Nation a sovereign nation. However, President Andrew Jackson refused to enforce the court's decision.

In 1838, federal troops were sent to forcibly relocate the Cherokee to Indian Territory (present-day Oklahoma). John Ross led his people on the arduous journey westward, but the conditions were deplorable. Thousands of Cherokees died from exposure, disease, and lack of resources during the forced migration. Despite Ross's efforts, the Cherokee Nation could not prevent the tragedy of the Trail of Tears.

A popular legend says that Ross's wife, known as Quatie, became ill after giving her coat to a crying child. While this story can't be verified, Quatie did die of pneumonia on the Trail of Tears.

Ross continued to advocate for the rights of the Cherokee people in Indian Territory, negotiating with the US government for compensation and the establishment of a new homeland. John Ross's leadership and dedication to his people's well-being during this tumultuous period make him a significant figure in American history.

25. The Mountain Men were rugged frontiersmen who roamed the American wilderness during the early 19th century, primarily in

the Rocky Mountains and other western regions. Hugh Glass was a mountain man and fur trapper who operated in the wilderness of the American West. His story is perhaps one of the most incredible survival tales of the American frontier.

In 1823, while on an expedition along the Grand River in South Dakota, Glass encountered a grizzly bear while hunting. The bear attacked him, severely mauling him and leaving him with life-threatening injuries. Despite his dire condition, Glass somehow managed to kill the bear with his flintlock rifle.

However, he was left alone and gravely wounded in the wilderness by his fellow trappers, who believed he had no chance of survival. With incredible determination, Glass crawled and dragged himself through the wilderness. He fashioned a makeshift stretcher from a broken rifle, and using it, he covered over two hundred miles over a period of six weeks, surviving on meager food and water.

Along his journey, Glass encountered various dangers, including encounters with Native American tribes. At one point, he was forced to fend off hostile Arikara, who had attacked him.

Ultimately, Glass reached the safety of Fort Kiowa, a trading post on the Missouri River, where he received medical attention. His story of survival became legendary in the American West and served as a testament to the indomitable spirit of the mountain men.

Although Hugh Glass's story has likely been embellished over the years, his tale of survival has inspired books, movies, and folklore, including the 2015 film *The Revenant*, which starred Leonardo DiCaprio in the role of Hugh Glass.

An illustration of Hugh Glass being attacked by a bear.

26. The Oregon Trail is one of American history's most iconic routes during the westward expansion. It was a challenging and arduous journey taken by thousands of pioneers in the mid-19th century as they sought new opportunities and a better life in the Oregon Territory.

The Oregon Trail was a roughly two-thousand-mile-long wagon route that began in Missouri and extended to the fertile valleys of Oregon. It was a grueling journey that often took several months, crossing challenging terrain, including deserts, mountains, and rivers.

One of the most tragic stories associated with westward expansion involves the Donner Party, a group of pioneers led by George and Jacob Donner. In the spring of 1846, they set out for California along a new route known as the Hastings Cutoff, which was supposed to be a shortcut. Unfortunately, the Hastings Cutoff turned out to be longer and more treacherous than expected. The Donner Party faced numerous hardships, including delays, dwindling supplies, and harsh weather in the

Sierra Nevada Mountains.

When they reached the Sierra Nevada in late October 1846, the Donner Party was ill-prepared for the harsh winter conditions. Trapped by deep snow, they were forced to camp at what is now known as Donner Lake.

As the winter wore on, the pioneers faced extreme hunger and starvation. Some members of the party resorted to cannibalism to survive. Rescue parties eventually reached the stranded pioneers in early 1847, but many had already perished.

The Oregon Trail and the Donner Party story are emblematic of the trials and tribulations faced by those who ventured west in pursuit of new opportunities and a better future during the era of westward expansion in the United States.

27. Frederick Douglass was born into slavery in Maryland around 1818 (his exact birthdate is not known). As a young boy, he endured the harsh conditions of slavery and the brutality of his masters.

At the age of around twenty, Douglass decided to escape from slavery. He devised a daring plan that involved borrowing the identification papers of a free African American sailor. With these papers, he disguised himself as a sailor and even wore a sailor's uniform while making his way to the train station in Baltimore.

Douglass's escape was filled with danger and uncertainty. He had to navigate various checkpoints and encounters with authorities who could have discovered his true identity at any moment. His courage and resourcefulness played a crucial role in his successful escape.

Eventually, he arrived in the free state of Pennsylvania and settled in New Bedford, Massachusetts. There, he adopted the name Frederick Douglass to avoid being recaptured.

Once free, Douglass became deeply involved in the abolitionist movement. He began attending anti-slavery meetings and soon became a powerful and captivating speaker, sharing his own experiences as a former slave and advocating for the abolition of slavery.

In 1845, he published his first autobiography, *Narrative of the Life of Frederick Douglass, an American Slave.* The book was a sensation and garnered attention both in the United States and abroad. However, its publication put Douglass at risk of being recaptured by slaveholders. To evade recapture, Douglass embarked on a tour of Ireland and the United Kingdom, where he continued to speak out against slavery. During this time, supporters raised money to purchase his freedom from his former owner, allowing him to return to the United States as a free man.

Frederick Douglass went on to become a prominent abolitionist leader, a staunch advocate for women's suffrage, and a distinguished writer and orator. His life story, from enslavement to freedom, remains a powerful and inspiring testament to the indomitable human spirit and the fight for justice.

28. The Seneca Falls Convention in 1848 marked a pivotal turning point in the history of women's rights, igniting a movement that would revolutionize the social and political landscape of the United States. At the heart of this movement were two remarkable women: Elizabeth Cady Stanton and Lucretia Mott.

Elizabeth Cady Stanton was a fiery orator and social reformer. She emerged as a leading voice for women's rights. Her impassioned speeches and written works challenged the prevailing notion that women were intellectually inferior and incapable of self-governance. Stanton believed that women possessed the same inherent rights as men and deserved equal opportunities in all aspects of life, including the right to vote.

Elizabeth married a prominent abolitionist, Henry Brewster Stanton. She took the word "obey" out of the marriage vows, later writing, "I obstinately refused to obey one whom I supposed I was entering into an equal relation." Although she took her husband's last name, she never referred to herself as Mrs. Henry Stanton, as was the custom at the time.

Alongside Stanton stood Lucretia Mott, a Quaker minister and abolitionist who brought her unwavering commitment to social justice to the women's rights movement. Mott's eloquence and moral authority resonated with the convention's attendees, inspiring them to demand a fundamental transformation of gender relations.

In 1840, Mott traveled to London to attend the World's Anti-Slavery Convention. Mott was a well-known advocate for the abolition of slavery and a firm believer in equal rights for all, regardless of gender. However, she faced a significant setback when she arrived at the convention. The male delegates at the World's Anti-Slavery Convention, despite their shared commitment to the abolitionist cause, refused to allow female delegates to participate. Mott was barred from speaking or participating in the proceedings solely based on her gender. Her experiences here led to the Seneca Falls Convention.

Together, Stanton and Mott crafted the Declaration of Sentiments, a bold manifesto that challenged the prevailing legal and social structure that subjugated women. The declaration boldly proclaimed, "All men and women are created equal," a radical assertion that defied the deeply entrenched patriarchal norms of the time.

29. In the early 19th century, educational opportunities for women in the United States were limited, with few options beyond elementary schooling. Mary Lyon, born in 1797 in Massachusetts, recognized the need for higher education for women. Lyon was deeply committed to the idea of providing women with access to a rigorous and comprehensive education. She was a dedicated teacher and worked to save money for her educational endeavors.

In 1834, Mary Lyon founded Mount Holyoke Female Seminary (now Mount Holyoke College) in South Hadley, Massachusetts. It was one of the first institutions of higher education exclusively for women in the United States.

What made Mount Holyoke particularly groundbreaking was its commitment to providing women with a rigorous curriculum that included advanced studies in subjects like mathematics, science, literature, and history. Lyon's vision was to prepare women not only for domestic roles but also for professions and careers.

Lyon was deeply involved in the seminary's day-to-day operations, serving as its founder and first principal. She was known for her dedication to the students and her high standards for education.

One of Mary Lyon's innovative ideas was to have students participate in the operation of the school as a way to reduce costs and make education more accessible. Students took on responsibilities such as cooking, cleaning, and farming as part of their education.

Mount Holyoke Female Seminary was successful and became a model for women's education. It inspired the founding of other women's colleges and played a crucial role in advancing women's access to higher education.

Mary Lyon's commitment to women's education and her pioneering efforts made her a trailblazer in the field. Her legacy lives on through Mount Holyoke College and the countless women who have benefited from the educational opportunities she championed.

30. The Mexican-American War lasted from 1846 to 1848. The US victory in the war expanded American territory significantly, with Mexico ceding present-day California, Nevada, Arizona, and more, setting the stage for further westward expansion and sparking debates over whether newly acquired territories would allow slavery or be free states.

Several prominent figures participated in the Mexican-American War, including Zachary Taylor, Winfield Scott, Ulysses S. Grant, Robert E. Lee, and "Stonewall" Jackson. *However, one group of people isn't as well known.*

A group of US Army soldiers known as the Saint Patrick's Battalion or the San Patricios fought in the Mexican-American War. This unit was largely composed of Irish and other European immigrants who had enlisted in the United States Army. During the Mexican-American War, some of these soldiers became disillusioned with the conflict, viewing it as an unjust invasion of Mexican territory. Motivated by a combination of anti-Catholic sentiment, mistreatment by their officers, and sympathy for the Mexican cause, a significant number of Irish soldiers defected from the US Army and joined the Mexican forces.

Under the leadership of John Riley (a deserter from the US military), the group fought against their former comrades. One notable engagement involving the San Patricios occurred during the Battle of Churubusco in August 1847. The San Patricios fought bravely against overwhelming odds but ultimately faced defeat. Many were captured, and a significant number were subsequently court-martialed and executed for desertion.

Despite the controversial nature of their actions, the San Patricios are remembered in both Mexican and Irish history as a group of individuals who found themselves torn between loyalties and ideologies during a turbulent period. The story of the Saint Patrick's Battalion serves as a reminder of the complex motivations and consequences of war, as well as the diverse backgrounds of those who participate in conflicts.

Section 4 – Forging a United Nation: The Crucible of 1850–1877

From 1850 to 1877, several significant events shaped the nation, including the Dred Scott decision and the secession of the Southern states, which started the Civil War.

This section looks at the lead-up to the Civil War, the war itself, and what happened afterward.

31. The Missouri Compromise of 1820 was an attempt to maintain a precarious balance between the slave and free states following Maine's petition for statehood. While it temporarily resolved the issue of statehood, the compromise inadvertently exacerbated sectional tensions and foreshadowed the looming Civil War.

    The admission of Missouri as a slave state and Maine as a free state was a delicate balancing act intended to preserve the equilibrium between the two factions. However, this perceived balance was deceptive, as the addition of Missouri further strengthened the South's political power and representation in Congress.

    In 1854, the Kansas-Nebraska Act was passed, which repealed the Missouri Compromise and allowed residents of those territories to decide the issue of slavery through popular vote. This decision sparked fierce clashes between pro-slavery and anti-slavery factions in Kansas. These clashes were aptly known as "Bleeding Kansas."

One battle of Bleeding Kansas saw only one accidental death. The sacking of Lawrence, Kansas, happened in 1856. Sheriff Samuel Jones went to Lawrence, which had been established by those who supported the end of slavery, to arrest settlers who supported abolition and were involved in a nearby conflict. Jones was driven out of the town, with people firing their guns at him.

As a result of this "assassination" attempt, a pro-slavery force attacked Lawrence. The pro-slavery forces ransacked the town, looting homes, destroying businesses, and setting fire to the Free State Hotel. One of the men from the pro-slavery faction died when a piece of the hotel fell on his head.

The sacking of Lawrence intensified the animosity between pro-slavery and anti-slavery factions in Kansas. It also contributed to the wider national tensions that eventually led to the outbreak of the American Civil War. The events in Lawrence underscored the bitter and violent nature of the struggle over the future of Kansas and the issue of slavery, foreshadowing the conflicts that would follow in the years leading up to the Civil War.

32. In 1857, Dred Scott, an enslaved man, ignited a national firestorm over slavery when he sued for his freedom after residing in free territories.

Dred Scott was born into slavery around 1795 in Virginia and later taken to the free state of Illinois and the Wisconsin Territory by his owner, Dr. John Emerson. In these regions, slavery was prohibited by the Missouri Compromise of 1820. After returning to Missouri, a slave state, Dred Scott and his wife Harriet filed lawsuits for their freedom based on the fact they had been living in territories where they were considered free.

The legal battle culminated in the infamous Supreme Court case *Dred Scott v. Sandford*. The Supreme Court, led by Chief Justice Roger B. Taney, delivered a controversial decision with far-reaching consequences. The Supreme Court ruled that enslaved individuals, even if taken to free territories, remained property and were not entitled to freedom or citizenship. Chief Justice Taney's opinion also declared the Missouri Compromise unconstitutional, arguing that Congress had no authority to prohibit slavery in the territories.

This decision heightened tensions and contributed to the growing divisions between the North and the South over the issue of slavery. The Dred Scott decision profoundly affected American society, exacerbating tensions that eventually led to the Civil War. It also played a role in the election of 1860, as the Republican Party, led by Abraham Lincoln, opposed the expansion of slavery into new territories.

The legacy of the Dred Scott case persisted even after the Civil War, influencing the drafting of the Fourteenth Amendment, which granted citizenship to all persons born or naturalized in the United States, regardless of race or previous condition of servitude. Today, the Dred Scott decision is considered one of the worst Supreme Court decisions in American history.

33. On October 16th, 1859, John Brown, an abolitionist, led a raid on the federal armory at Harpers Ferry, Virginia, in an attempt to spark a slave uprising. He attempted to get several renowned abolitionists to join him, such as Frederick Douglass and Harriet Tubman, *but both declined.*

Brown believed hundreds of slaves would join his cause. However, he had no way of contacting slaves on nearby plantations. He wasn't willing to give up the cause, though.

The first casualty of the raid was a freed Black man who had been shot from behind by one of the raiders on October 17th. The Lost Cause movement, which arose in 1866 and focused on the Confederacy fighting for states' rights, not slavery, claimed the man who had been shot was for slavery remaining in the states.

Brown and his men would go on to capture several hostages and hold them in the armory's fire engine house. The raid was quickly suppressed by a combined force of local militia and US Marines led by Colonel Robert E. Lee. Stonewall Jackson and Jeb Stuart, talented military officials on the Confederacy's side during the Civil War, also helped put down the raid.

Brown and his men were captured on October 18th. Brown was tried for treason and murder and was executed on December 2nd, 1859. John Wilkes Booth, who would go on to kill President Abraham Lincoln, witnessed Brown's death by hanging.

In the North, Brown's raid was considered a heroic act of defiance against slavery. Abolitionists

hailed Brown as a martyr, and his actions inspired many to join the anti-slavery movement. However, others in the North were horrified by the violence and condemned Brown's actions.

In the South, Brown's raid fueled fears of a slave insurrection and intensified Southern resentment toward the North. Many Southerners believed the raid was part of a larger plot by abolitionists to destroy their way of life. This belief further solidified Southern determination to protect slavery, even if it came to war.

34. Fort Sumter is located in the harbor of Charleston, South Carolina. In 1860, it was one of the last remaining federal military installations in the South under Union control. In December 1860, South Carolina seceded from the Union, followed by several other Southern states. However, Fort Sumter remained under Union control – a clear source of tension between the North and the South.

President James Buchanan's administration tried to resupply and reinforce the fort peacefully. However, negotiations with South Carolinian authorities stalled, and the situation became increasingly volatile. On April 6th, 1861, Confederate Brigadier General P. G. T. Beauregard, in command of Confederate forces in Charleston, was ordered by the Confederate government to demand the surrender of Fort Sumter. Major Robert Anderson, the Union commander of the fort, refused to surrender, but he was running low on supplies and ammunition.

On April 12th, 1861, Confederate forces opened fire on Fort Sumter, beginning a thirty-four-hour bombardment. This marked the start of the American Civil War. The Union garrison at Fort Sumter fought back, but they were outmatched, and the fort suffered significant damage.

On April 13th, Major Anderson and his men surrendered. Remarkably, there were no fatalities during the bombardment, although one Union soldier died and three were injured while firing a salute during the Union's evacuation.

The fall of Fort Sumter galvanized both the North and the South. President Abraham Lincoln called for seventy-five thousand volunteers to suppress the rebellion, leading to the mobilization of Union forces and the escalation of the Civil War. Fort Sumter remained in Confederate hands for most of the war but was eventually recaptured by Union forces in 1865.

35. The Civil War has many interesting stories. One of them involves a general named Benjamin Butler. In May 1861, three enslaved men – Frank Baker, James Townsend, and Shepard Mallory – escaped from Confederate-held territory in Virginia and sought refuge at Fort Monroe, a Union stronghold in Virginia commanded by General Butler. When their owner, Colonel Charles Mallory, demanded the return of his "property," General Butler faced a dilemma.

Butler had been a lawyer before the war and recognized that returning the escaped men to the Confederate forces would essentially mean aiding the enemy. So, he deemed the three men "contraband of war," arguing they were being used by the Confederacy to support its war effort.

This decision set a precedent for the Union's treatment of escaped slaves. The term "contraband" became widely used, and other Union commanders adopted Butler's approach. As more enslaved individuals sought refuge behind Union lines, the North's policy evolved, setting the stage for a shift in the Union's stance on slavery.

While the Emancipation Proclamation had not been issued at that point, the contraband policy marked a significant step toward the eventual emancipation of enslaved people. President Abraham Lincoln issued the Emancipation Proclamation on January 1st, 1863, declaring all enslaved individuals in Confederate-held territory to be free. Four states (Delaware, Maryland, Kentucky, and Missouri) retained slavery until the end of the war and the passage of the Thirteenth Amendment in 1865.

President Abraham Lincoln sought to preserve the unity of the Union and prevent further secession by not challenging slavery in these border states. He believed that emancipation in these states would alienate them and push them into the

Confederacy. These border states were also situated between the Union and the Confederacy, making them crucial for controlling the flow of goods, troops, and information.

While the Emancipation Proclamation didn't immediately free all enslaved people, it changed the character of the Civil War by making the abolition of slavery a central war aim. The story of the contraband policy at Fort Monroe illustrates how individual actions and decisions by military commanders, such as General Benjamin Butler, can play a role in shaping the broader trajectory of a war.

36. The Battle of Gettysburg is known for several key moments, one of which is Pickett's Charge, a Confederate assault led by General George Pickett on the final day of the battle, July 3rd, 1863.

General George Pickett was a Confederate division commander known for his distinctive appearance, including his long, jet-black beard. He was tasked with leading a desperate and ill-fated assault against the center of the Union lines on Cemetery Ridge. Pickett's Charge involved approximately twelve thousand Confederate soldiers who marched across an open field toward the Union positions while enduring devastating artillery and rifle fire.

The charge was a valiant but ultimately unsuccessful effort to break the Union lines. Confederate forces suffered heavy casualties, and the charge is often considered the high-water mark of the Confederacy.

General Pickett himself narrowly escaped death during the charge. As he rode his horse toward the front lines, he was injured when his horse was shot out from under him. Pickett was knocked unconscious but survived, though he was deeply affected by the loss of his men.

After the failed charge, General Pickett reportedly met with General Robert E. Lee, the Confederate commander, who took responsibility for the defeat and expressed his regret for ordering the ill-fated assault.

General George Pickett's name became forever associated with the charge, and he would carry the weight of that association for the rest of his life. He later referred to the charge as "the slaughter pen." The Union victory at Gettysburg is often seen as a turning point in the war.

37. On April 9ᵗʰ, 1865, General Robert E. Lee surrendered to General Ulysses S. Grant, effectively ending the Civil War and beginning the process of rebuilding and reconciliation.

The owner of the home where Grant and Lee met, Wilmer McLean, had moved to Appomattox after his first house was partially destroyed in the war's first major battle, the First Battle of Bull Run, in 1861. McLean allegedly said, "The war began in my front yard and ended in my front parlor."

The Union forces would take several objects from the home, such as the table used to sign the surrender. They paid McLean hundreds of dollars for these priceless artifacts. However, some items were simply stolen.

Grant was overcome with emotion when he saw Lee at the surrendering table. The two talked of the Mexican-American War, which they had fought together on the same side. General Grant would give Lee generous terms of surrender. Lee's men would not be imprisoned for treason. They could keep their sidearms and horses, and Grant gave them food.

General Grant's decision to grant generous terms of surrender to Lee and his army was a strategic move aimed at minimizing further bloodshed and promoting reconciliation. He instructed his troops to treat the Confederates with respect and dignity, avoiding any acts of retribution. Grant's magnanimous treatment of Lee extended to the personal interactions between the two generals.

During their meeting at the McLean House in Appomattox, Grant allowed Lee to retain his sword, a symbol of his military rank and honor. While seemingly insignificant, Lee deeply appreciated this gesture, and served as a powerful symbol of respect and reconciliation.

The treatment of Lee at Appomattox was not merely an act of military courtesy; it was a conscious decision to promote healing and unity in a nation torn apart by war.

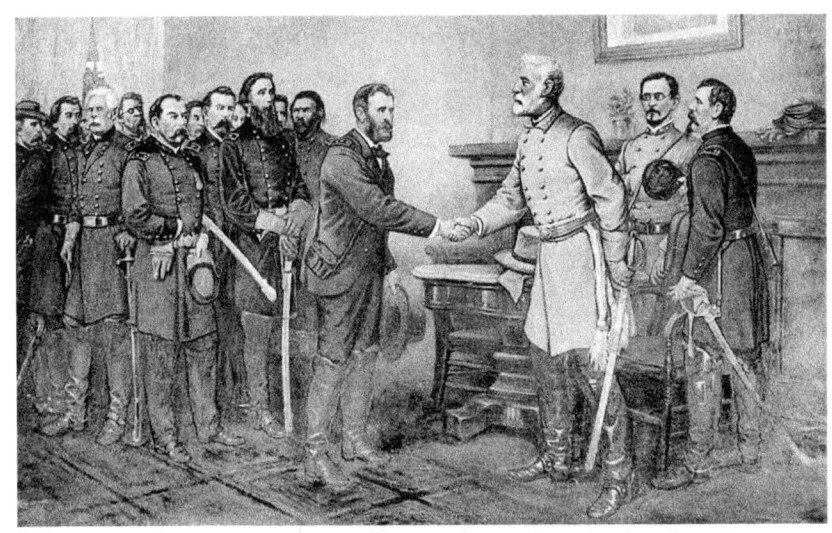

Lee surrendering to Grant at the Appomattox Court House.

38. The Thirteenth Amendment abolished slavery in the United States. Its passage marked a decisive turning point in the nation's history, ending the legalized institution of slavery that had entrenched itself for centuries. The amendment's impact extended beyond the immediate liberation of enslaved people, setting the stage for further advancements in civil rights and equality.

    Thaddeus Stevens, a fiery congressman from Pennsylvania, played a crucial role in abolishing slavery in the United States. His sharp tongue and political maneuvering earned him the title "The Old Commoner," and his influence in the Republican Party proved critical in pushing through the Thirteenth Amendment.

    Stevens's personal life was complex, and his relationship with his Black housekeeper, Lydia Hamilton, added further layers to his legacy. While Stevens never publicly declared their status, some historians believe they maintained a long-term, loving relationship. They lived together for decades, and Stevens financially supported her and their daughter.

    However, speculating on the intimate nature of their relationship risks historical overreach. Instead, it's crucial to recognize the ambiguity surrounding their bond while acknowledging Stevens's unwavering commitment to racial equality. He openly challenged racial prejudice, championed voting rights for Black Americans, and fiercely condemned Jim Crow laws.

Stevens's dedication to abolition wasn't solely fueled by political expediency. He genuinely believed in human equality, a conviction honed over decades of fighting injustice. While his personal life remains shrouded in some mystery, his contribution to ending slavery in the United States remains undeniable.

39. Most people have heard of John Wilkes Booth. But have you ever heard of a woman named Mary Surratt?

During the American Civil War, Mary Surratt was a boarding house owner in Washington, DC. She became linked to the assassination of President Abraham Lincoln through her son, John Surratt, and her boarding house's association with John Wilkes Booth, the assassin.

John Wilkes Booth, a Confederate sympathizer and actor, hatched a plot to assassinate President Lincoln, Vice President Andrew Johnson, and Secretary of State William H. Seward. On the evening of April 14th, 1865, Booth shot President Lincoln at Ford's Theatre while the president was attending a play.

Mary Surratt's son, John Surratt, was involved in the conspiracy and had connections to Booth. He had participated in earlier discussions about kidnapping President Lincoln but was not directly involved in the assassination itself.

After the assassination, Booth fled Washington, DC, and a massive manhunt was launched to capture him and his co-conspirators. Mary Surratt and others were suspected of conspiring with Booth. On April 17th, 1865, Mary Surratt was arrested at her boarding house. During the subsequent trial by a military commission, she was accused of providing aid and shelter to Booth and his co-conspirators, even though she maintained her innocence.

Mary Surratt's trial was controversial. On June 30th, 1865, she was found guilty and sentenced to death. Mary Surratt was hanged alongside three other convicted conspirators on July 7th, 1865. She was the first woman in US history to be executed by the federal government.

Her execution was met with mixed reactions, with some believing she was a willing participant in the plot and others sympathizing with her as a mother who may have been unaware of her son's activities. Her conviction and execution remain the subject of historical debate, as some argue that her role in the conspiracy may not have warranted the death penalty.

40. Hiram Revels was born in Fayetteville, North Carolina, in 1827 to free parents of African and Native American descent. In 1866, during the Reconstruction era following the Civil War, Revels became a minister in the African Methodist Episcopal Church. Soon after, he entered politics. He was appointed an alderman in Natchez, Mississippi, becoming one of the first African Americans to hold a public office in the South.

In 1867, Mississippi was readmitted to the Union under the Reconstruction Acts, and the state's legislature elected Hiram Revels to the US Senate in 1870. Revels became the first African American to serve in the US Senate and the US Congress.

Revels served as a US senator from Mississippi from February 25th, 1870, to March 3rd, 1871. While in the Senate, he advocated for civil rights, education, and equality for African Americans. One of Revels' most notable speeches in the Senate was his response to a speech by Senator Charles Sumner of Massachusetts. Sumner argued for the desegregation of public schools, and Revels supported his position by sharing the progress made toward racial equality in Mississippi.

Revels's service in the Senate was met with both praise and hostility, with some of his fellow senators opposing his presence due to his race. Despite the challenges, he conducted himself with dignity and integrity.

After his term in the Senate, Revels continued to be involved in education and ministry. He became the first president of Alcorn Agricultural and Mechanical College (now Alcorn State University) in Mississippi, a historically Black institution.

Hiram Revels's legacy extends beyond his time in office. He paved the way for other African Americans to serve in Congress and contributed to advancing civil rights and education during the Reconstruction era. Although the Reconstruction era did not end positively for Black Americans, with the Jim Crow laws being passed in the South, his legacy as a pioneering figure in American history continues to be celebrated today.

Section 5 – From Rails to Rights: Transformative Events in the Late 19th and Early 20th Centuries

Important events unfolded in America during the late 19th and early 20th centuries. Explore events like the Great Railroad Strike, the Spanish-American War, and the Triangle Shirtwaist Factory fire. The Progressive era brought sociopolitical changes, and the suffrage movement culminated in the Nineteenth Amendment.

There is a lot to uncover from this period, so let's get started!

41. The Great Railroad Strike of 1877 began in Martinsburg, West Virginia, when workers for the Baltimore and Ohio Railroad (B&O) went on strike on July 16th, 1877. The strike was sparked by a wage cut for B&O railroad workers, who were already facing challenging working conditions and low pay.

    Frustration among the workers had been building for years. As the strike in Martinsburg escalated, it quickly spread to other cities and railroad hubs along the B&O line, including Baltimore, Maryland, and Pittsburgh, Pennsylvania. Soon, railroad workers from other companies joined the strike as well.

    The strike became one of the largest and most violent labor uprisings in US history. Striking workers blocked rail lines, sabotaged equipment, and clashed with police and state militias. In Baltimore, the strike took a particularly violent turn. Rioting erupted as striking workers clashed with the Maryland National Guard. Troops fired into the crowd, resulting in numerous deaths and injuries. The strike continued to spread to other states, including Illinois and Missouri, where additional railroads were affected, leading to further confrontations and violence.

President Rutherford B. Hayes eventually intervened, sending federal troops to quell the unrest. The use of federal troops marked one of the earliest instances of federal military intervention in a labor dispute in the United States. The strike gradually subsided as federal troops and state militias gained control of the situation. By early August 1877, the strike had effectively ended.

While the strike did not achieve its immediate goals of wage increases and improved working conditions for railroad workers, it did bring attention to labor issues and set the stage for future labor movements and the growth of labor unions in the United States.

42. The Dawes Act of 1887 authorized the US government to break up Native American tribal lands into individual allotments, with the goal of assimilating Native Americans into mainstream American society. Its consequences included the loss of traditional lands and cultural identity among Native American communities.

Prior to the Dawes Act, the Osage Nation had negotiated treaties that secured their territory in what is now Oklahoma. However, the discovery of oil on Osage lands in the late 19th century intensified pressure for assimilation and land division. Under the Dawes Act, the Osage Reservation was allotted to individual tribal members, and the surplus land was opened to non-native settlers.

What makes the Osage story particularly significant is the oil found in their lands. The Dawes Act inadvertently made the Osage among the wealthiest people per capita in the world at the time due to the discovery of oil reserves. Each tribal member received an allotment, including mineral rights, which led to lucrative oil leases.

In response to this wealth from oil, the US government implemented a system whereby non-indigenous guardians were appointed to manage the financial affairs of some of the Osage, especially those deemed "incompetent" to handle their wealth. This system led to widespread corruption and exploitation, with some guardians siphoning off the Osage people's wealth.

The Osage became victims of a series of murders. Several Osage women were killed by their White husbands for money. Most of the murders from this period were never solved.

This tragic series of events highlighted the vulnerability of indigenous communities in the face of external exploitation. Eventually, in the 1920s, the Osage Nation and the federal government worked together to address the corruption and injustice. The Osage murders became the FBI's first major homicide investigation.

43. Rising tensions between the US and Spain, fueled by newspaper sensationalism and the explosion of the USS *Maine*, led to the Spanish-American War. Although the explosion of the USS *Maine* is an interesting story, we are going to take a look at what future President Theodore Roosevelt was up to.

The Rough Riders was a volunteer cavalry regiment led by Colonel Theodore Roosevelt. The regiment was a diverse mix of cowboys, miners, lawmen, and college athletes, and it also included a notable contingent of African American soldiers. The Rough Riders gained fame for their role in the Battle of San Juan Hill, which took place on July 1ˢᵗ, 1898, near Santiago de Cuba.

During the battle, the Rough Riders and other US forces faced well-entrenched Spanish positions on San Juan Hill. The attack was intense, with heavy fire from Spanish troops positioned in blockhouses and trenches. The Rough Riders, led by Roosevelt, and the Buffalo Soldiers, an African American regiment, played key roles in the uphill assault. One of the most iconic moments of the battle was the charge up Kettle Hill and San Juan Hill.

As the Rough Riders and other US forces advanced, Roosevelt led the charge on horseback, becoming a symbol of American courage and determination. Contrary to the name, the Rough Riders, for the most part, didn't use horses. The horses had been left behind in the US due to some confusion.

Nevertheless, the Rough Riders fought valiantly. Their involvement in the Battle of San Juan Hill received extensive media coverage, and their exploits were celebrated back in the United States. Theodore Roosevelt's leadership during the battle significantly contributed to his political rise, and he later became the vice president and then president of the United States.

The Spanish-American War had far-reaching consequences. The US emerged victorious, gaining Puerto Rico, Guam, and the Philippines. The acquisition of territories propelled the United States onto the global stage, expanding its influence beyond its borders and establishing it as a major power. This newfound status ushered in a period of increased involvement in international affairs, with the United States taking on a more assertive role in shaping the world order.

44. "Soapy" Smith, whose real name was Jefferson Randolph Smith II, was a notorious American con artist and crime boss who operated during the late 19th and early 20th centuries. He became infamous for his schemes and criminal activities in various parts of the United States, including the Klondike Gold Rush in Alaska and the frontier town of Skagway, Alaska.

Soapy Smith was born in Coweta County, Georgia, on November 2nd, 1860. He grew up in a family of con artists and learned the tricks of the trade from a young age. Soapy was a master of confidence tricks, shell games, and other forms of deception.

He often operated in towns that were experiencing rapid growth due to the Klondike Gold Rush, where newcomers were eager for entertainment and opportunities but also vulnerable to scams. Soapy Smith is perhaps best known for his activities in Skagway, Alaska, during the Klondike Gold Rush. He and his gang established a criminal empire in the town, a major gateway for prospectors heading to the goldfields of the Yukon.

Soapy and his gang controlled Skagway through a combination of fraud, intimidation, and violence. He established a telegraph office and used it to intercept messages – gaining valuable information about newcomers and their wealth. Soapy's gang, known as the "Soap Gang," engaged in various illegal activities, including rigged gambling games, fake lotteries, and extortion. He and his henchmen would often target vulnerable newcomers, swindling them out of their money.

Soapy Smith's reign in Skagway eventually drew the attention of law enforcement and vigilantes who were determined to clean up the town. In July 1898, a confrontation known as the "Shootout on Juneau Wharf" occurred between Soapy's gang and a group of vigilantes led by Frank Reid. Soapy Smith was fatally wounded in the shootout and died the next day.

Soapy Smith's life and criminal activities have been the subject of numerous books, articles, and even a few films. His name is often associated with the era of frontier lawlessness and the challenges of maintaining order in rapidly growing, lawless towns.

An image of Soapy Smith.

45. Before Upton Sinclair's 1906 novel *The Jungle* shed searing light on the American meatpacking industry, darkness reigned in the nation's stockyards. Chicago's Packingtown, a sprawling complex of slaughterhouses and processing plants, hummed with the unglamorous industry churning out meat for a hungry nation. Yet, beneath the surface of economic prosperity lurked a grim reality for the men and women who kept the gears turning.

These workers, drawn by the promise of steady wages, predominantly hailed from countries like Lithuania, Poland, and Germany. Their diverse languages and backgrounds collided in the cacophony of the kill floor. But shared hardships forged a grim camaraderie. Their days were brutal: long hours in damp, fetid conditions amidst the constant thud of cleavers, the stench of blood and offal, and the ever-present threat of injury from unforgiving machinery.

Safety was a fleeting privilege, sacrificed for expediency. Fingers were lost to unguarded saws, limbs became tangled in gears, and exhaustion blurred vision, leading to countless cuts and gashes. Illness bloomed from the filth and fumes, affecting the health of workers already weakened by malnutrition and meager pay.

Greed dictated every corner of the operation. Meat deemed unfit for human consumption was repackaged and sold, tainted products disguised with chemicals and preservatives. The workers, deemed replaceable cogs in the machine, lived in cramped, squalid housing, preyed upon by landlords and saloon keepers.

Sinclair, posing as a Lithuanian immigrant, plunged into this world for seven weeks. His fictional protagonist, Jurgis Rudkus, became a vessel for the collective suffering he witnessed. Jurgis's descent from hopeful newcomer to broken man mirrored the fate of countless real-life workers. Through him, Sinclair exposed the industry's gruesome underbelly – the callous disregard for worker safety, the rampant adulteration of food, and the exploitation of vulnerable immigrants.

The book's impact was immediate and visceral. Public outcry forced President Theodore Roosevelt to launch an investigation, leading to the passage of the Pure Food and Drug Act and the Meat Inspection Act of 1906. While these reforms didn't eradicate all problems, they marked a turning point, forcing the industry to acknowledge its responsibility for worker safety and food quality.

46. On March 25th, 1911, a devastating fire broke out at the Triangle Shirtwaist Factory in New York City. The factory was located on the eighth, ninth, and tenth floors of the Asch Building in Manhattan.

The Triangle Shirtwaist Factory was a clothing sweatshop where predominantly immigrant women and girls worked long hours in unsafe conditions. The workers produced shirtwaists (blouses) for women.

The fire started on the eighth floor, likely due to a discarded cigarette or a faulty sewing machine, and quickly spread. The factory's doors were locked to prevent theft and unauthorized breaks, trapping workers inside. The lack of fire safety measures, such as sprinklers and fire escapes, made it difficult for workers to escape the rapidly advancing fire. The fire department's ladders could not reach the upper floors of the building.

In a desperate attempt to escape the flames, some workers jumped from the windows to their deaths on the pavement below. Others were burned alive or asphyxiated in the smoke-filled rooms. The fire lasted only about 18 minutes but resulted in the deaths of 146 people, the majority of whom were young immigrant women, many of them Jewish and Italian.

The Triangle Shirtwaist Factory fire shocked the nation. It galvanized the labor reform movement and led to increased awareness of workers' rights and the need for improved safety conditions in factories. In the aftermath of the fire, public outcry and increased activism for workers' rights and safety reforms led to legislative changes in New York State and eventually nationwide. These reforms included improved fire safety regulations, worker compensation laws, and the establishment of factory inspection agencies.

47. The women's suffrage movement gained momentum during the Progressive era, with women demanding the right to vote. The efforts of suffragettes and other organizations led to the passage and enactment of the Nineteenth Amendment in 1919 and 1920, respectively, granting women the right to vote.

However, it was not smooth sailing. At the forefront of the women's suffrage movement were activists known as the Silent Sentinels. They picketed the White House, demanding the right to vote for women. Many of these suffragists were arrested and, following their arrests, endured harsh conditions in prison.

On November 14th, 1917 (also known as the Night of Terror), a group of thirty-three suffragists, including Lucy Burns and Alice Paul, were transferred to the Occoquan Work House, where they were subjected to brutal treatment by prison guards. The women were beaten, verbally abused, and force-fed when they went on hunger strikes to protest their imprisonment.

One of the most infamous incidents involved the treatment of Alice Paul, who was placed in a straitjacket, tied to her cell bars, and left for hours. Other suffragists faced similar brutality, with some being thrown into cold, unsanitary cells and denied basic necessities.

News of the Night of Terror spread rapidly, drawing attention to the suffragists' cause and intensifying public support for women's suffrage. The harsh treatment faced by these activists helped expose the brutality of the authorities and contributed to a shift in public opinion.

All of the suffragists involved in the Night of Terror were released by November 27th. It would only take two months for President Woodrow Wilson – who was blamed for the cruelty – to announce a bill on women's suffrage.

An image of the Silent Sentinels protesting outside the White House

48. President Theodore Roosevelt is well known for his reforms in office. However, let's break up our stories of the reforms made during the Progressive era and focus on something a little different.

In November 1902, President Theodore Roosevelt embarked on a hunting expedition in Mississippi, guided by a famous Mississippi bear hunter named Holt Collier. The expedition aimed to hunt black bears, which were prevalent in the area. After days of hunting, the party had little success, and President Roosevelt was eager to find a bear to shoot.

On November 14th, the hunting dogs cornered a black bear. Roosevelt approached the bear but was troubled by its exhausted and defenseless condition. He considered it unsportsmanlike to shoot the bear in such a state. Instead of shooting the bear, Roosevelt ordered that it be put out of its misery with a knife, ending the hunt without shooting the bear.

News of President Roosevelt's act of compassion spread quickly, and it captured the public's imagination. A political cartoonist named Clifford Berryman depicted the scene in a cartoon titled "Drawing the Line in Mississippi," published in *The Washington Post* on November 16th, 1902. The cartoon portrayed Roosevelt refusing to shoot the bear, and this image soon became iconic.

The bear in the cartoon was depicted as a small, cuddly bear cub, which later inspired a Brooklyn candy shop owner named Morris Michtom. Morris Michtom's wife, Rose, had the idea to create a stuffed bear toy based on the cartoon. They called it the teddy bear, combining Roosevelt's nickname, "Teddy," with "bear."

The teddy bear became a sensation and quickly gained popularity. The teddy bear's popularity led to the establishment of the Ideal Novelty and Toy Company by the Michtoms, and it became a beloved children's toy.

The compassion displayed by Theodore Roosevelt during the bear hunt inspired the creation of the teddy bear and cemented his reputation as a compassionate leader.

49. In the early 20th century, the United States faced a series of financial panics and banking crises. One of the most significant of these crises occurred in 1907, known as the Panic of 1907. The Panic of 1907 was characterized by a severe financial downturn,

bank runs, and a lack of centralized control over the nation's monetary system. The absence of a central bank made it challenging to respond effectively to the crisis.

The panic was largely triggered by the attempt to manipulate the stock price of the United Copper Company, leading to a chain reaction of bank runs and financial instability. Prominent banker and financier J. P. Morgan played a key role in stemming the panic. Morgan personally organized a group of fellow bankers who pooled their resources to support troubled banks and restore confidence in the financial system.

While Morgan's efforts helped stabilize the situation, they also highlighted the need for a more systematic and permanent solution to financial crises and the regulation of the banking system. In the wake of the Panic of 1907, there was a growing consensus that the United States needed a central banking system to provide stability, regulate the money supply, and act as a lender of last resort during financial crises.

In 1913, President Woodrow Wilson signed the Federal Reserve Act into law, creating the Federal Reserve System. The Fed was established as a decentralized central bank with twelve regional banks and a Board of Governors in Washington, DC. The Federal Reserve was given the authority to issue currency, set interest rates, regulate banks, and provide a safety net during financial emergencies.

It became the cornerstone of the United States' modern monetary and financial system. Over the years, the Federal Reserve has played a crucial role in managing the country's monetary policy, responding to financial crises, and fostering economic stability.

50. The construction of the Panama Canal, a monumental engineering feat, was completed in 1914. This waterway connected the Atlantic and Pacific Oceans, significantly reducing ship travel time and enhancing international trade and transportation. The canal facilitated global trade and commerce and projected American engineering prowess and strategic dominance on the world stage. This engineering marvel solidified America's position as a major player in international affairs, ushering in an era of American dominance for most of the 20th

century.

One interesting story related to the Panama Canal involves the successful efforts to combat and eradicate mosquito-borne diseases during its construction. Malaria and yellow fever were major health threats to workers during the early attempts to build the Panama Canal, particularly during the French construction efforts in the late 19th century. The French project, led by Ferdinand de Lesseps, faced significant challenges, including high worker mortality rates due to these diseases.

When the United States took over canal construction in the early 20th century, Chief Engineer John F. Stevens and later Chief Engineer George W. Goethals implemented a comprehensive public health campaign to address mosquito-borne diseases. The campaign was led by Dr. William C. Gorgas, a US Army surgeon and sanitation expert. Gorgas and his team focused on controlling the mosquito population, which transmitted diseases like malaria and yellow fever. They implemented measures such as draining standing water, fumigating buildings, and introducing larvicide to kill mosquito larvae.

One of the most significant breakthroughs was the discovery that the *Aedes aegypti*, also known as the yellow fever mosquito, was the primary vector for yellow fever. By eliminating the breeding grounds of this specific mosquito, Gorgas and his team drastically reduced the incidence of yellow fever.

The successful control of mosquito-borne diseases was crucial for completing the Panama Canal. The improved public health conditions allowed for a steady and efficient workforce. The canal was officially opened on August 15th, 1914. The efforts to combat disease during the construction of the Panama Canal were pioneering in the field of tropical medicine and contributed to advancements in public health practices worldwide.

Section 6 – From Victories to Superpower: The Transformative Years of 1914–1945 in American History

From 1914 to 1945, important events shaped American history. The Roaring Twenties brought economic growth, but the Great Depression brought economic decline. The US entered World War II after the attack on Pearl Harbor, ultimately dropping atomic bombs on Hiroshima and Nagasaki, setting the stage for the Cold War.

Let's look at some interesting stories from American history during this pivotal era in the modern age.

51. As Europe geared up for the cataclysm of World War I, a different conflict simmered across the Rio Grande. The years leading to America's 1917 entry into the global war were marked by escalating tensions with Mexico, a turbulent mix of revolutionary unrest, border skirmishes, and clashing personalities.

    The embers of this tension were ignited by the Mexican Revolution, a bloody struggle for social justice that erupted in 1910. American interests, particularly mining and oil companies, found themselves caught in the crossfire. Raids across the border by revolutionary factions led by charismatic figures like Pancho

Villa became commonplace, stoking fears of instability and threats to American lives and property.

President Woodrow Wilson, a pacifist at heart, navigated this volatile landscape with cautious neutrality. He recognized the legitimacy of Mexican aspirations for reform but worried about escalating violence and safeguarding American interests. This balancing act proved increasingly difficult as border attacks, particularly Villa's raid on Columbus, New Mexico, in 1916, became bolder and more brazen.

Enter General John Pershing, a rising star in the US Army. Wilson, pressured by public outrage and congressional demands for action, sent Pershing across the border with a mission to capture Villa and restore order. The "Punitive Expedition," as it was called, became a frustrating exercise in cat-and-mouse pursuit. Pershing, a meticulous planner, struggled to track down the elusive Villa in the vast Mexican desert, while Mexican President Venustiano Carranza vehemently opposed the incursion of his nation's sovereignty.

Meanwhile, a young George Patton, serving under Pershing, honed his tactical skills and thirst for action. Though the expedition failed to capture Villa, it served as a training ground for the American military, preparing them for the larger conflict to come.

Ultimately, America's entry into World War I in 1917 drew focus away from the Mexican border. The Punitive Expedition was withdrawn, leaving behind a simmering discontent and a reminder of the complex and often fraught relationship between the two nations.

52. During World War I, the United States remained neutral for the initial years of the conflict while Germany waged unrestricted submarine warfare against Allied shipping. In January 1917, British intelligence intercepted a coded telegram sent by the German foreign minister Arthur Zimmermann to the German ambassador in Mexico, Heinrich von Eckardt.

The Zimmermann Telegram proposed a military alliance between Germany and Mexico in the event that the United States entered World War I on the side of the Allies (Britain, France, and Russia, among others). Germany promised Mexico financial support and the return of territory lost to the United States, specifically Texas, New Mexico, and Arizona.

British codebreakers successfully decrypted the telegram and shared its contents with the United States in late February 1917. The revelation of the Zimmermann Telegram had a profound impact on the United States. It aroused public outrage and significantly influenced public opinion regarding the war.

On April 2nd, 1917, President Woodrow Wilson asked Congress for a declaration of war against Germany, stating that the world must be made safe for democracy. The United States officially entered World War I on April 6th, 1917.

American involvement in the war played a critical role in tipping the balance in favor of the Allies and ultimately contributed to their victory. The Zimmermann Telegram is often cited as a pivotal event that led to the United States' entry into World War I.

After the war, German officials confirmed the authenticity of the Zimmermann Telegram, further cementing its historical significance. The Zimmermann Telegram is a compelling example of how intelligence and diplomacy intersected during World War I. Its interception and disclosure demonstrated the power of codebreaking in warfare.

53. The Roaring Twenties was a period of economic prosperity and cultural change, characterized by the introduction of new technologies, jazz music, and social liberation. However, this era was also marred by the passage of the Eighteenth Amendment, which prohibited the production, sale, and transportation of liquor.

While intended to promote temperance, Prohibition had the unintended consequence of giving rise to a thriving illegal alcohol trade and the emergence of powerful criminal organizations. One of the most notorious figures of this era was Al Capone, also known as "Scarface." Capone rose to prominence as a gangster and bootlegger in Chicago, where he controlled a significant portion of the illegal alcohol trade. His criminal empire included speakeasies, breweries, and a network of corrupt officials. Capone's operation was highly organized, and he became known for his ruthlessness in eliminating rivals and maintaining control over his territory. His criminal activities extended beyond alcohol, involving racketeering, gambling, and other illicit enterprises.

Despite the violence associated with Capone and his gang, he managed to cultivate a public image as a charismatic and generous figure. For instance, in response to the economic hardships faced by many Americans during the Great Depression, Al Capone decided to establish soup kitchens to provide free meals to those in need. These soup kitchens, often organized by Capone's associates, distributed food to Chicago's unemployed and impoverished individuals.

Capone's motivations for these charitable efforts were likely complex. Some speculate that he saw this as a way to improve his public image, especially given the negative attention he received for his criminal activities. Additionally, the economic hardships of the Great Depression presented an opportunity for Capone to gain favor among the public.

The story of Al Capone and the Prohibition era provides a window into the complex and often contradictory dynamics of a transformative period in American history. To this day, the Eighteenth Amendment is the only amendment in the US Constitution to be repealed. Prohibition ended in 1933.

Al Capone in 1930.

54. In 1927, Charles Lindbergh achieved one of the greatest feats in aviation history when he became the first person to fly solo nonstop across the Atlantic Ocean. This historic flight earned him international acclaim and forever marked his place in the annals of aviation.

On May 20th, 1927, Lindbergh took off from Roosevelt Field in New York on his solo journey to Paris, France. Lindbergh's flight covered a distance of approximately 3,600 miles (5,800 kilometers). He navigated primarily using dead reckoning and celestial navigation. The flight lasted thirty-three hours and thirty minutes.

Lindbergh landed at Le Bourget Field in Paris on May 21st, 1927, to a hero's welcome. A crowd of 100,000 people gathered to greet him, and he became an instant international sensation. Lindbergh received numerous awards and honors for his achievement, including the Orteig Prize, which offered a $25,000 reward for the first nonstop transatlantic flight.

Charles Lindbergh's life took a dark turn in 1932. Charles Lindbergh Jr., the twenty-month-old son of Charles Lindbergh and his wife, Anne Morrow Lindbergh, was kidnapped from the family's home in Hopewell, New Jersey. The Lindbergh baby abduction became a sensational and high-profile case, ultimately leading to one of the most famous criminal investigations in American history.

On the night of March 1st, 1932, the Lindbergh baby was taken from his nursery through an open window. A handwritten ransom note demanding $50,000 was left behind.

The Lindberghs complied with the ransom demands and initiated negotiations with the kidnapper, who used a series of coded letters and phone calls to communicate. The ransom was paid, but the baby was not returned.

Tragically, in May 1932, the baby's remains were found in a wooded area about 4.5 miles from the Lindbergh home. An autopsy determined that the child had died from a fractured skull.

The investigation led to the arrest of Bruno Hauptmann, a German immigrant who had some of the ransom money in his possession. Hauptmann was tried, found guilty of kidnapping and murder, and subsequently executed in the electric chair in 1936. To this day, people are unsure if Hauptmann was guilty.

The Lindbergh baby kidnapping case had a profound impact on American law, leading to the Federal Kidnapping Act, also known as the "Lindbergh Law," which made kidnapping a federal offense if the victim was taken across state lines. It also heightened security measures and awareness surrounding child safety.

55. On October 29th, 1929, the stock market crashed, marking the beginning of the Great Depression, the worst economic downturn in American history. The Great Depression, which spanned from 1929 to the late 1930s, was a period of unprecedented economic hardship in the United States. The stock market crash of 1929 triggered a devastating domino effect, leading to widespread unemployment, business failures, and financial ruin. The nation's industrial heartland was particularly hard-hit, as factories shuttered and workers lost their jobs. Farmers struggled with plummeting crop prices and harsh weather conditions while poverty and hunger became rampant.

After World War I, Congress passed legislation promising a bonus to veterans, but the payment was not scheduled until 1945. As the Great Depression deepened, many veterans found themselves in dire economic circumstances. In response, a group of approximately 20,000 veterans, known as the *Bonus Expeditionary Force* or *Bonus Army*, marched to the nation's capital in the summer of 1932 to demand immediate payment of their bonuses. The veterans set up makeshift camps in and around Washington, DC, hoping to draw attention to their cause. They occupied government buildings, including abandoned federal buildings and an area across from the Capitol known as Anacostia Flats. The Bonus Army hoped to influence Congress to pass legislation for early payment of their bonuses.

As the summer progressed, tensions rose, and the situation became more contentious. The veterans faced resistance from local authorities. President Herbert Hoover ordered the evacuation of the Bonus Army's camps. On July 28th, 1932, the US Army, led by General Douglas MacArthur and Major Dwight D. Eisenhower, both of whom would play important roles in

World War II, forcibly removed the veterans from their camps. Tear gas and military force were used to disperse the protesters.

The eviction of the Bonus Army was a highly publicized and controversial event. The images of the US military confronting World War I veterans garnered widespread attention and contributed to the negative public perception of President Hoover's handling of the economic crisis.

The Bonus Army clash with the police in 1932.
https://commons.wikimedia.org/wiki/File:Bonus_marchers_05510_2004_001_a.gif

56. During the Great Depression of the 1930s, Hoovervilles – makeshift shantytowns that housed homeless and unemployed Americans – sprang up in various cities across the United States. One of the most well-known Hoovervilles was located in New York City, right in the heart of Manhattan's Central Park.

This Hooverville, often called the "Central Park Hooverville," was established in the early 1930s. Central Park's Hooverville was home to hundreds of homeless individuals and families who had lost their jobs, homes, and savings due to the economic hardships of the Great Depression. Residents of Central Park Hooverville constructed their homes from whatever materials they could find, such as cardboard, wood scraps, and metal. The shacks and tents were densely packed into the area, forming a makeshift community.

Life in Central Park Hooverville was challenging, with residents lacking access to basic amenities like running water and sanitation facilities. The community faced overcrowding, poor hygiene, and inadequate shelter, but it provided a sense of community and support for its inhabitants.

In addition to the dire living conditions, residents faced the constant threat of eviction. City officials and park authorities often attempted to clear Hooverville, viewing it as an eyesore and a violation of park regulations.

Central Park Hooverville became a symbol of the economic suffering and homelessness caused by the Great Depression. Photographers and journalists documented life in Hooverville, bringing attention to the plight of the homeless during this challenging period.

As the country slowly emerged from the Great Depression and implemented relief programs under President Franklin D. Roosevelt's New Deal, conditions in Hoovervilles gradually improved. Central Park Hooverville was eventually dismantled in the mid-1930s, but its existence serves as a lasting reminder of the economic hardship and social challenges faced by Americans during the Great Depression.

57. On December 29th, 1940, Roosevelt announced that the United States would be the "Arsenal of Democracy," pledging to provide military aid and support to countries fighting against the Axis powers in World War II. The US became a major supplier of war material, contributing significantly to the eventual victory of the Allies. The USA gave the USSR over 400,000 trucks alone.

Yes, although the US and Russia are often at odds today, the two were allies during World War II. As part of the Lend-Lease program, the United States provided military aid to the Soviet Union, which was a crucial partner on the Eastern Front against Nazi Germany.

One remarkable aspect of the Lend-Lease program was the aircraft deliveries to the Soviet Union through the use of a route known as the Alaska-Siberia (ALSIB) airway. This airway allowed American-made aircraft to be flown from the United States to the Soviet Union, crossing over Alaska and Siberia.

Pilots, many of whom were civilian aviators, played a crucial role in delivering the aircraft. They flew the planes across the treacherous terrain of Alaska and the vast distances of Siberia, facing extreme weather conditions, long flights, and challenging navigation.

One of the notable aircraft delivered through the ALSIB route was the Bell P-39 Airacobra. This single-engine fighter aircraft, equipped with a unique mid-mounted cannon, became an important asset for the Soviet Air Force on the Eastern Front.

The ALSIB route witnessed hundreds of successful deliveries of American aircraft to the Soviet Union during the war. The cooperation through the Lend-Lease program, including the daring flights of the ALSIB route, strengthened the Allied effort against the Axis powers and showcased the global scale of collaboration during World War II.

58. On December 7th, 1941, Pearl Harbor was attacked by the Japanese, prompting the United States to enter World War II. Needless to say, the attack on Pearl Harbor was a pivotal moment in American history, marking the nation's entry into World War II and shaping its foreign policy for decades to come. The immediate ramifications of the attack were devastating, with over two thousand Americans killed, hundreds wounded, and seven ships sinking.

During the surprise attack by the Japanese, the USS *Nevada* was moored at Battleship Row on the southern side of Ford Island. The ship was one of the primary targets and suffered several bomb hits and torpedo strikes. Despite being heavily damaged, the crew of the USS *Nevada*, under the command of Captain Francis W. Scanland, managed to get the ship underway.

Realizing that the battleship was in danger of sinking and blocking the harbor entrance, Captain Scanland ordered the USS *Nevada* to head for the open sea. Under intense enemy fire, the ship made a daring attempt to escape the harbor. Despite sustaining further damage and being targeted by Japanese aircraft, the USS *Nevada* successfully navigated the harbor channel. The crew intentionally beached the battleship on Hospital Point to prevent it from sinking in the harbor entrance.

The grounding of the USS *Nevada* had strategic implications. It allowed the ship to avoid obstructing the harbor and allowed the US to salvage and eventually repair it. In the aftermath of the attack, the USS *Nevada* was repaired, modernized, and returned to active service in the Pacific theater later in the war.

The story of the USS *Nevada*'s attempt to escape during the attack on Pearl Harbor showcases the determination, resourcefulness, and bravery of the Americans under challenging circumstances. The ship's successful grounding and subsequent recovery became a symbol of resilience in the face of adversity during one of the darkest days in American military history.

The USS Nevada in 1944.

58. The United States dropped atomic bombs on the Japanese cities of Hiroshima and Nagasaki in early August 1945, leading to Japan's surrender and the end of World War II.

While it is difficult to know for sure, it is believed the atomic bombings of Hiroshima and Nagasaki resulted in an estimated 129,000 to 226,000 Japanese deaths, with the majority of the casualties occurring in the immediate aftermath of the explosions. The bombings also caused widespread injuries and long-term health effects, including radiation sickness and cancer.

In 1955, ten years after the bombing, a group of twenty-five Japanese women who had survived the atomic blast sought medical help in the United States to address severe disfigurements and scars caused by the radiation. The Japanese women were victims of the long-term effects of the atomic bomb, facing physical and social challenges due to their appearance.

A humanitarian effort was launched to bring these women to the United States for medical treatment and reconstructive surgery. The initiative was led by Dr. Tatsuo Yamada, a Japanese plastic surgeon, and journalist Norman Cousins, who helped coordinate the project. The undertaking was named the Hiroshima Maidens program.

The Hiroshima Maidens arrived in the United States in 1955, where they received medical care, surgeries, and rehabilitation at Mount Sinai Hospital in New York City. The treatment aimed to improve both their physical health and their social well-being by addressing the visible effects of the atomic bomb.

The story of the Hiroshima Maidens gained significant media attention, and the women became symbols of the long-term consequences of nuclear warfare. The program provided medical care and facilitated cultural exchange and understanding between the Japanese survivors and the American medical community.

59. In the late 1940s, after the successful testing of atomic bombs in the New Mexico desert, the Manhattan Project continued its research to improve the design and efficiency of these weapons. One critical component of the atomic bomb was a sphere of fissile material, usually plutonium or uranium, that could sustain a nuclear chain reaction when brought to a critical mass. This core was often referred to as the "pit."

In August 1945, a few days before the bombing of Nagasaki, physicist Harry Daghlian was conducting experiments at the Los Alamos Laboratory in New Mexico. He was working with a plutonium core, later known as the "demon core." Daghlian was performing a critical experiment to measure the effects of placing tungsten carbide bricks around the plutonium core, essentially testing how close the core could come to achieving a critical mass without causing a nuclear chain reaction. Daghlian accidentally dropped a brick onto the plutonium core during the experiment, causing it to go *supercritical.*

Neutron radiation flooded the room, and Daghlian quickly realized the danger he was in. With heroic effort, Daghlian removed the brick and attempted to limit his radiation exposure, but it was late; he had received a lethal dose of radiation during the incident.

Daghlian was rushed to the hospital, and despite the best efforts of medical staff, he died twenty-five days later on September 15th, 1945, becoming the first known fatality directly attributed to radiation exposure from a criticality accident.

The "demon core" was involved in another criticality accident less than a year later when physicist Louis Slotin conducted a similar experiment. Slotin also died from radiation exposure, further emphasizing the dangers of working with fissile materials.

These incidents contributed to increased awareness of the hazards of nuclear research and the need for strict safety protocols in nuclear facilities. They also played a role in the development of safety measures and procedures for handling fissile materials.

Section 7 –America's Journey from 1946 to 1980

From 1946 to 1980, various pivotal events shaped American history. The Cold War tensions between the US and the Soviet Union set the stage with proxy wars like the Korean War and the Vietnam War. *Brown v. Board of Education* deemed school segregation unconstitutional, fueling the civil rights movement. The Watergate scandal and Nixon's resignation exposed corruption.

Explore this period with a look at some interesting stories!

60. The Marshall Plan was a US program that provided aid to Western Europe following the devastation of World War II. Enacted in 1948, it provided over fifteen billion dollars to help finance rebuilding efforts in Europe. The plan aimed to restore economic stability, prevent the spread of communism, and foster economic interdependence between Europe and the United States.

    After World War II, France faced severe economic challenges, including a crippled industrial base, food shortages, and a struggling economy. The Marshall Plan played a crucial role in helping France rebuild and revitalize its economy. One notable example is the transformation of the French city of Le Havre.

    Le Havre had suffered extensive damage during the war, and its port - critical for trade and economic activity, was in ruins.

The city was selected as a recipient of Marshall Plan aid. Under the leadership of Auguste Perret, a French architect, Le Havre underwent a remarkable reconstruction project. Perret adopted innovative urban planning and architectural techniques, including the use of reinforced concrete, to rebuild the city quickly and efficiently. The reconstruction of Le Havre became a showcase for modern urban design and post-war recovery.

In 1950, Le Havre was officially unveiled as a shining example of the successful implementation of the Marshall Plan. The rebuilt city featured wide streets, modern buildings, and a revitalized port. The transformation of Le Havre symbolized not only the physical reconstruction of war-torn Europe but also the economic and social revival made possible by the Marshall Plan.

61. In 1950, North Korean forces invaded South Korea, leading to a three-year conflict. The US and other allies intervened to support South Korea against communist aggression. The Korean War was a proxy war between the United States and the Soviet Union, contributing to the Cold War tensions.

One notable battle from this war took place in Inchon. Inchon is a port city on the west coast of Korea. During the war, it was heavily fortified and considered an unlikely location for an amphibious invasion due to its challenging tidal conditions. The tides in Inchon were among the highest in the world, with a range of up to thirty-six feet, making it a risky and unconventional choice for an amphibious assault.

Against the advice of many military advisors, General Douglas MacArthur, the Supreme Commander of the United Nations Command, devised a plan to launch a surprise attack on Inchon. The operation, codenamed Operation Chromite, aimed to cut off North Korean forces and relieve the pressure on United Nations forces, which had been pushed to the Pusan Perimeter in the southeastern part of the Korean Peninsula.

On September 15th, 1950, UN forces launched a bold amphibious assault on Inchon. The operation's success relied on precise timing to take advantage of the narrow window when the tides were at their highest. The element of surprise, combined with the audacity of attacking such a challenging location, caught the North Korean forces off-guard.

The amphibious assault at Inchon proved to be a masterstroke, as the UN forces quickly secured the city and began to turn the tide of the war. The successful operation is often credited with altering the course of the Korean War in favor of the UN forces.

Ultimately, the Korean War would end in a stalemate. Some believe the two sides remained in a frozen conflict since no peace treaty that marked the end of the war was ever signed. Nevertheless, the Battle of Inchon remains a remarkable example of military strategy and bold decision-making, showcasing General MacArthur's leadership and the effectiveness of well-executed amphibious operations in unconventional environments.

62. Linda Brown was a third-grader in Topeka, Kansas. She had to walk a considerable distance to her segregated Black school, even though there was a white school much closer to her home. Her father, Oliver Brown, became frustrated with the unequal educational opportunities available to his daughter and decided to take action. In 1950, Oliver Brown, along with several other African American parents, filed a class-action lawsuit against the Board of Education of Topeka, Kansas.

Their case, combined with other cases from Delaware, South Carolina, Virginia, and Washington, DC, was consolidated into what became known as *Brown v. Board of Education*. The plaintiffs argued that racial segregation in public schools was a violation of the Fourteenth Amendment, which guarantees equal rights to all citizens.

The case was argued before the Supreme Court in 1952 and 1953. In 1954, the Supreme Court, in a unanimous decision, ruled in favor of the plaintiffs, declaring that state laws establishing separate public schools for Black and White students were unconstitutional. The landmark decision in *Brown v. Board of Education* overturned the precedent set by the 1896 case *Plessy v. Ferguson*, which upheld the concept of "separate but equal" facilities for different races.

Linda Brown, though just a child at the time of the case, became a symbol of the fight against racial segregation in education. The *Brown v. Board of Education* decision marked a pivotal moment in the civil rights movement and set the stage for dismantling segregation in all areas of public life in the United States. The legacy of this case continues to influence discussions about equal access to education and civil rights.

63. On December 1ˢᵗ, 1955, Rosa Parks, a seamstress and civil rights activist, was riding a bus in Montgomery, Alabama, after a long day of work. She was seated in the "colored" section of the bus, which was the racially segregated seating arrangement enforced in the city.

As the bus continued its route, it became crowded, and some White passengers were left standing. The bus driver, James F. Blake, demanded that Rosa Parks and three other African American passengers give up their seats to White passengers. Rosa Parks made a courageous decision to refuse to give up her seat to a White man, which was against the city's segregation laws.

Parks's act of civil disobedience led to her arrest and subsequent charges of violating segregation laws. She was taken into custody by the police and spent the night in jail. News of her arrest spread quickly, sparking outrage and mobilizing the African American community in Montgomery.

Leaders of the Montgomery Improvement Association (MIA), including a young minister named Martin Luther King Jr., organized a boycott of the city's buses in protest of Parks's arrest and racial segregation on public transportation. The Montgomery bus boycott, as it became known, lasted for 381 days. African Americans in Montgomery refused to ride the city's buses, causing a significant financial strain on the transportation system. The boycott's success caught the attention of the nation and the world, drawing support from civil rights activists, sympathizers, and leaders across the country.

In 1956, the United States Supreme Court ruled in the case of *Browder v. Gayle* that racial segregation on Montgomery buses was unconstitutional, effectively ending segregation on public transportation in the city. Rosa Parks's courage and the Montgomery bus boycott marked a turning point in the civil rights movement. Her actions and the subsequent legal victory demonstrated the power of nonviolent protest and grassroots activism.

Rosa Parks in 1955. You can see Martin Luther King Jr. in the background.

64. During the height of the Cold War, the United States conducted extensive surveillance missions over the Soviet Union to gather intelligence. The U-2 spy plane was a crucial tool in these efforts due to its high-altitude capabilities.

On May 1st, 1960, a U-2 spy plane piloted by Francis Gary Powers took off from Pakistan on a reconnaissance mission to photograph Soviet military installations. The mission, codenamed Operation Grand Slam, aimed to gather valuable intelligence about the Soviet Union's nuclear capabilities.

While flying over Soviet airspace, Powers's U-2 plane was detected and tracked by Soviet radar. Despite the aircraft's high altitude, it was eventually hit by a surface-to-air missile. Powers's

U-2 was brought down, and he was captured by Soviet authorities.

Powers survived the crash and was taken into custody. Initially, the US government claimed that the U-2 was a weather reconnaissance plane that had gone off course and inadvertently strayed into Soviet territory. However, the Soviet Union presented evidence of the espionage mission, including photos taken by Powers's camera equipment.

The U-2 incident caused a major diplomatic crisis between the United States and the Soviet Union. The Soviets accused the US of conducting espionage flights, which the US initially denied but later admitted.

Powers was put on trial in the Soviet Union and sentenced to ten years in prison for espionage. He spent over a year in captivity before being exchanged for Soviet spy Rudolf Abel in a high-profile prisoner exchange on the Glienicke Bridge in Berlin in 1962.

The U-2 incident prompted increased scrutiny of US reconnaissance efforts and the development of alternative surveillance methods. However, the U-2 spy plane remained in service and played a role in subsequent intelligence-gathering missions during the Cold War and beyond.

65. The Cuban Missile Crisis of 1962 was a tense standoff between the United States and the Soviet Union over the presence of Soviet nuclear missiles in Cuba, which is just ninety miles off the coast of Florida.

To gather crucial intelligence about the missile installations in Cuba, the United States conducted reconnaissance flights using U-2 spy planes. These high-altitude flights allowed the US to monitor the situation and provide photographic evidence to the world.

On October 27th, 1962, during the height of the crisis, U-2 pilot Major Rudolf Anderson Jr. was on a reconnaissance mission over Cuba. He was flying at an altitude of 70,500 feet, well above the range of Soviet surface-to-air missiles. Despite the altitude, Soviet generals ordered a surface-to-air missile to be fired at Anderson's U-2 plane. The missile struck the aircraft, causing it to disintegrate and killing Anderson. He became the only combat casualty of the Cuban Missile Crisis.

Rudolf Anderson's tragic death underscored the extremely high stakes of the Cuban Missile Crisis and the dangers faced by those involved in intelligence-gathering missions. His sacrifice served as a poignant reminder of the need for accurate information and diplomacy during times of international crisis. It also contributed to the resolution of the crisis, as it became clear that a peaceful solution was preferable to the potentially catastrophic consequences of nuclear war.

The Cuban Missile Crisis was eventually resolved through negotiations, with the US agreeing to remove its missiles from Turkey and the Soviets agreeing to dismantle their missile installations in Cuba.

66. Dr. Martin Luther King Jr. was a central figure in the civil rights movement and played a crucial role in advocating for the passage of the Civil Rights Act of 1964.

In the early 1960s, Dr. King and other civil rights leaders organized a series of nonviolent protests, including sit-ins, marches, and voter registration drives, to challenge segregation and discrimination in the United States. These protests, particularly the Birmingham campaign in 1963, drew national attention and placed immense pressure on the federal government to address civil rights issues.

On August 28th, 1963, Dr. King delivered his iconic "I Have a Dream" speech during the March on Washington for Jobs and Freedom, which took place at the Lincoln Memorial in Washington, DC. His powerful and inspiring words resonated with millions of Americans and helped galvanize support for civil rights legislation.

President John F. Kennedy was initially cautious about pushing for comprehensive civil rights legislation, fearing backlash from Southern segregationist lawmakers. However, the momentum of the civil rights movement and the moral imperative became increasingly evident.

Tragically, President Kennedy was assassinated on November 22nd, 1963. His successor, President Lyndon B. Johnson, recognized the need to honor Kennedy's legacy and moved forward with civil rights legislation.

President Johnson, who had served in the Senate and understood how to navigate the legislative process, used his political skills to push for the Civil Rights Act of 1964. He also used his relationship with lawmakers to secure their support for the bill. On July 2nd, 1964, President Johnson signed the Civil Rights Act into law. The act prohibited discrimination on the basis of race, color, religion, sex, or national origin, and it ended segregation in public places and banned employment discrimination.

Dr. Martin Luther King Jr.'s leadership and the grassroots efforts of countless activists nationwide played a significant role in creating the public demand for the Civil Rights Act. The passage of the Civil Rights Act of 1964 marked a historic step toward dismantling institutional racism and advancing civil rights in the United States. It remains a landmark piece of legislation in American history.

67. On July 20th, 1969, NASA's Apollo 11 mission achieved the historic feat of landing two astronauts, Neil Armstrong and Edwin "Buzz" Aldrin, on the lunar surface. Michael Collins remained in orbit around the moon aboard the command module.

As the lunar module *Eagle* descended to the moon's surface, Neil Armstrong, the mission's commander, took control of the spacecraft. The situation became tense as they encountered a rocky and uneven landing site with only seconds of fuel remaining. Armstrong's exceptional piloting skills allowed him to manually maneuver the spacecraft, avoiding a potentially catastrophic landing. With just twenty-five seconds of fuel left, Armstrong safely touched down on the moon's surface.

The historic moment occurred when Neil Armstrong descended the lunar module's ladder and became the first human to set foot on the moon. He famously said, "That's one small step for man, one giant leap for mankind." The quote was intended to convey the significance of this achievement for all of humanity. However, it is often misquoted as "That's one small step for a man," with the "a" making the sentence grammatically complete. Armstrong maintained that he had said "a" during the transmission but acknowledged that it might not have been clearly audible due to radio static.

Regardless of the exact wording, Armstrong's first step on the moon was an extraordinary moment that captivated the world and marked a historic milestone in space exploration. Buzz Aldrin joined Armstrong on the lunar surface, and together, they conducted experiments, planted the American flag, and collected lunar samples during their two-and-a-half hours outside the lunar module.

The successful return of Apollo 11's astronauts to Earth on July 24th, 1969, marked the conclusion of this historic mission and a monumental achievement in human exploration. The Apollo 11 moon landing remains one of the most iconic events in human history, representing the pinnacle of human achievement in space exploration. Neil Armstrong's famous words as he stepped onto the lunar surface continue to inspire generations and remind us of the incredible capabilities of science and technology.

Buzz Aldrin salutes the American flag.

68. The Vietnam War, spanning from 1955 to 1975, marked a tumultuous period in American history, characterized by escalating US involvement in a highly controversial conflict that ignited widespread protests and demonstrations. This divisive war, rooted in the Cold War struggle between communism and democracy, saw the US embroiled in a protracted and costly military effort to support South Vietnam against communist North Vietnam and its allies.

   In December 1972, the United States was engaged in negotiations with North Vietnam to end the war. However, peace talks had reached an impasse, and President Richard Nixon decided to take drastic measures to push for a resolution. On December 18th, 1972, Operation Linebacker II began, later called the "Christmas Bombing."

   Over the course of eleven days, from December 18th to December 29th, the US conducted an intensive bombing campaign targeting Hanoi and Haiphong in North Vietnam. The objective was to force North Vietnam back to the negotiating table by inflicting significant damage on its infrastructure and military capabilities. The bombing campaign involved the use of B-52 Stratofortress bombers and other aircraft, dropping a massive number of bombs on the designated targets. The scale and intensity of the bombings were unprecedented, with the US dropping over twenty thousand tons of bombs during this period.

   The Christmas Bombing had a profound impact on both North Vietnam and the international community. It caused widespread destruction and civilian casualties, drawing criticism from around the world. The intense public reaction and diplomatic pressure contributed to the resumption of peace talks.

   Remarkably, despite the devastation caused by the bombings, peace talks resumed in January 1973, leading to the signing of the Paris Peace Accords later that month. The accords paved the way for the withdrawal of US forces from Vietnam and established a ceasefire. The Christmas Bombing, while controversial and heavily criticized, played a role in ultimately bringing about a negotiated end to the Vietnam War.

69. The Watergate scandal began with a break-in at the Democratic National Committee headquarters in the Watergate complex in

Washington, DC, on June 17th, 1972. The burglars were caught, leading to an investigation.

Two investigative reporters, Bob Woodward and Carl Bernstein of *The Washington Post*, played a crucial role in uncovering the scandal. Their reporting exposed a series of illegal activities, including the break-in and a subsequent cover-up by the Nixon administration.

What made their investigation even more intriguing was the mysterious source known as "Deep Throat." Deep Throat was a high-ranking official within the US government who provided Woodward and Bernstein with crucial information, guidance, and leads related to the Watergate scandal. Deep Throat insisted on remaining anonymous and communicated with the reporters in secret meetings in parking garages. His information was instrumental in connecting the dots and unraveling the extent of the scandal.

For more than thirty years, Deep Throat's identity remained one of the greatest mysteries in American journalism and politics. Speculation and theories about his identity persisted. In 2005, it was revealed that W. Mark Felt, an associate director of the FBI during the Watergate era, was Deep Throat. Felt's decision to provide confidential information to the reporters was driven by his concern for the integrity of the FBI and his belief that the truth about Watergate needed to be exposed. The revelation of Deep Throat's identity added a new layer of historical significance to the Watergate scandal and solidified his place in American political history.

The Watergate scandal ultimately led to the resignation of President Richard Nixon on August 8th, 1974, as he faced imminent impeachment by Congress. Vice President Gerald Ford succeeded Nixon as president. Ford would go on to pardon Nixon, ending any chance of an indictment.

Section 8 – Shaping the Nation: From Reaganomics to the Oklahoma City Bombing

From 1981 to the early 2000s, several important events and developments shaped American history. Technological advancements, such as the introduction of personal computers, revolutionized the way people lived and worked. The fall of the Berlin Wall in 1989 marked the end of the Cold War and signified a major shift in global dynamics. Cultural shifts and tragic incidents like the Los Angeles riots and the Oklahoma City bombing highlighted the ongoing challenges and complexities faced by the United States during this period.

Let's see how the nation was shaped during this era.

70. President Ronald Reagan, often dubbed the "Great Communicator," wove humor into his speeches and debates with the ease of a seasoned storyteller. His quips weren't fiery punchlines but rather gentle nudges, disarming audiences with self-deprecating wit and playful jabs at opponents.

    In a debate about his age, Reagan chuckled, "I have no intention of running for President of the United States when I'm 73. My current plan is to be Governor of California for four more years, then go do some movies, or maybe write a book, then retire and watch all the ball games I want." This self-aware deflection deflected potential age concerns with a dose of charm.

He eventually did go on to run for president– *a race he won!*

Reagan reveled in poking fun at himself. Describing the arduous budget process, he once joked, "The budget process is much like a pregnant elephant. All the excitement happens in the dark, and the result is rather large and ungainly." This down-to-earth humor resonated with audiences, painting him as relatable and approachable.

Reagan's humor wasn't just a sideshow; it served a purpose. It disarmed tension, endeared him to audiences, and helped him articulate complex ideas in memorable ways. His gentle wit became a signature style that cemented his image as a folksy leader with a twinkle in his eye and a mischievous grin.

Unfortunately, Reagan's sense of humor sometimes got him into trouble. For instance, on August 11th, 1984, during a radio address preparation session at his California ranch, while testing the microphone, Reagan said, "My fellow Americans, I'm pleased to tell you today that I've signed legislation that will outlaw Russia forever. We begin bombing in five minutes."

Though intended as a lighthearted joke, this off-the-cuff remark was picked up by the microphone and later leaked to the public. It caused a stir on both sides of the Iron Curtain, with the Soviet Union condemning the statement as irresponsible and Reagan's opponents in the upcoming presidential election criticizing it as a sign of poor judgment.

71. On March 30th, 1981, President Ronald Reagan was leaving the Washington Hilton Hotel after delivering a speech. As he exited the hotel and approached his limousine, shots were fired. John Hinckley Jr., a mentally unstable individual, fired six shots in an attempt to assassinate President Reagan. Hinckley was armed with a .22 caliber revolver and had a history of stalking actress Jodie Foster, which played a role in his motivation for the attack.

President Reagan was hit by one of the bullets, which punctured his left lung and came close to his heart. White House Press Secretary James Brady, a Secret Service agent, and a District of Columbia police officer were also injured in the shooting. In the chaos that followed, Secret Service agents quickly reacted to protect the president and rushed him to the hospital. The swift medical response and surgery saved Reagan's life.

Reagan's famous humor and resilience emerged even amid a life-threatening situation. As he was wheeled into the operating room, he reportedly joked to the medical team, "I hope you're all Republicans."

The assassination attempt prompted a nationwide outpouring of support for President Reagan. He received thousands of get-well messages and letters from people across the country. John Hinckley Jr. was arrested at the scene and later found not guilty by reason of insanity during his trial. The verdict led to significant changes in laws regarding the insanity defense.

President Reagan recovered from his injuries and continued to serve as president of the United States for the remainder of his two terms, from 1981 to 1989. The attempted assassination had a lasting impact on presidential security procedures, leading to increased security measures for future presidents.

A picture of Reagan just before he was shot.

72. Have you ever wondered how computers began to impact our lives? On August 12th, 1981, IBM unveiled the IBM 5150, the first personal computer (PC) to gain widespread adoption. This groundbreaking innovation marked the dawn of the PC

revolution, transforming how people worked, communicated, and entertained themselves. The IBM PC's open architecture and compatibility with a vast array of software applications fueled its popularity, paving the way for the creation of a thriving personal computing industry.

In 1984, Apple launched the Macintosh computer, a revolutionary product that marked a significant departure from the text-based interfaces of earlier computers. The Macintosh featured a graphical user interface with icons, windows, and a mouse – a design inspired by the work done at Xerox PARC (Palo Alto Research Center) in the 1970s.

The story begins with Xerox PARC, where researchers developed a revolutionary graphical user interface, *Alto*. This system incorporated the use of a mouse and graphical elements, allowing users to interact with the computer more intuitively. Xerox, however, failed to capitalize on the potential of this groundbreaking technology.

In a twist of fate, Steve Jobs, co-founder of Apple, visited Xerox PARC in 1979 and saw the Alto in action. Recognizing the immense potential of the graphical user interface, Jobs initiated the development of a similar system for Apple's upcoming computer, the Macintosh.

The Macintosh, introduced in January 1984, featured a 9-inch monochrome display, a 3.5-inch floppy disk drive, and an affordable price tag compared to other graphical systems at the time. The Macintosh's graphical user interface, combined with its marketing campaign, which included the famous *1984* Super Bowl commercial, made it a standout product.

The Macintosh's release had a profound impact on the personal computer industry. It set new standards for user-friendly designs and influenced the development of future operating systems. Computers were made more accessible to a broader audience, shaping how people interact with technology. The legacy of the Macintosh continues to influence computing and user interface design to this day.

73. The Space Shuttle Challenger was a part of NASA's Space Shuttle program and made its maiden flight on April 4th, 1983. It was designed to carry astronauts and payloads into space.

On January 28th, 1986, the Challenger was set to launch from the Kennedy Space Center in Florida on mission STS-51-L. This mission was significant because it included the first private citizen selected to fly in space. Christa McAuliffe, a high school social studies teacher from New Hampshire, was chosen from thousands of applicants to be the first private citizen and teacher in space as part of NASA's Teacher in Space Project. Her selection was intended to promote the importance of education and space exploration.

Millions of Americans and people worldwide watched the Challenger launch live on television. However, just seventy-three seconds after liftoff, the shuttle broke apart, resulting in the tragic deaths of all seven crew members. The disaster was caused by the failure of an O-ring seal in one of the solid rocket boosters, which led to the explosion of the external fuel tank.

The Challenger explosion had a profound impact on the space program and raised questions about the safety of the Space Shuttle fleet. NASA suspended the Space Shuttle program for over two years while investigations were conducted and safety improvements were implemented.

Christa McAuliffe's dream of becoming the first teacher in space was tragically cut short, but her legacy endured. Her memory inspired further dedication to space exploration and education. In 1998, NASA launched the Christa McAuliffe Fellowship Program to honor her legacy and support teachers in their professional development.

The Challenger explosion remains a somber and significant chapter in the history of space exploration. It serves as a reminder of the risks and challenges associated with human spaceflight and the dedication of those who pursue the frontiers of science and discovery.

74. On June 12th, 1987, during a visit to West Berlin, President Ronald Reagan delivered a historic and memorable speech at the Brandenburg Gate, a prominent location near the Berlin Wall. President Reagan addressed the divided city of Berlin in his speech, directly challenging the Soviet leader, Mikhail Gorbachev, and the East German government. He declared, "Mr. Gorbachev, open this gate! Mr. Gorbachev, tear down this

wall!"

President Reagan's words were a clear and unequivocal call for the removal of the Berlin Wall, a powerful symbol of the division between East and West Germany. At the time, some advisors had urged Reagan to avoid making such a direct and confrontational statement, fearing it might harm relations with the Soviet Union. However, Reagan insisted on including these iconic words in his speech.

The speech was received with enthusiasm by West Berliners, who saw it as a powerful expression of Western solidarity and a message of hope for reunification. While the Berlin Wall did not come down immediately following Reagan's speech, it added pressure and brought international attention to the issue of the wall's existence.

Two years later, in 1989, a series of events, including peaceful protests, led to the fall of the Berlin Wall. The removal of the wall marked a pivotal moment in history, and the subsequent reunification of East and West Germany followed in 1990.

President Reagan's "Tear Down This Wall" speech is remembered as a powerful statement of American leadership, principles, and commitment to the cause of freedom. It remains an iconic moment in the history of the Cold War.

75. Operation Desert Storm was the US-led military campaign that aimed to liberate Kuwait from Iraqi occupation during the Gulf War (1990–1991). On January 16th, 1991, the US and its coalition allies launched a massive air campaign against Iraq, targeting military installations, communication centers, and strategic targets. This marked the beginning of the aerial phase of Operation Desert Storm. The coalition included countries such as the United Kingdom, France, Saudi Arabia, and many others, with the United States providing the bulk of the military forces.

One of the most iconic moments of the Gulf War was the live coverage of the conflict by CNN. Journalist Peter Arnett, reporting from Baghdad, provided real-time updates and images of the airstrikes, bringing the war into living rooms worldwide.

On February 24th, 1991, the coalition launched a ground offensive to retake Kuwait. US Army General H. Norman Schwarzkopf, the commander of the coalition forces, orchestrated the campaign. The US military employed innovative tactics during the ground offensive, including the "left hook" strategy, which involved a flanking maneuver by the US and coalition forces to encircle and defeat the Iraqi Army.

The ground offensive was highly successful, and within a few days, Kuwait was liberated from Iraqi forces. The coalition had achieved its primary objective.

Following a hundred hours of ground combat, the Gulf War ended with a ceasefire on February 28th, 1991. Iraq's military capabilities were significantly degraded, but Saddam Hussein remained in power.

The US and its coalition allies demonstrated the effectiveness of a coordinated, multinational military force in addressing international conflicts. The Gulf War had a lasting impact on US military doctrine and operations, influencing future strategies and military engagements.

76. On March 3rd, 1991, Rodney King, an African American man, was brutally beaten by four Los Angeles Police Department officers after a high-speed chase. The incident was captured on amateur video by a witness and later widely broadcast on television. The footage showed King being repeatedly struck with batons, kicked, and subjected to other forms of excessive force, even though he appeared to offer no resistance.

The video ignited outrage and brought attention to issues of police brutality and racial injustice. When the officers involved were acquitted in a state criminal trial in April 1992, it sparked widespread protests and civil unrest in Los Angeles. The riots, which began on April 29th, 1992, lasted for several days and resulted in significant property damage, injuries, and loss of life.

Reginald Denny, a White truck driver, became another focal point of the riots after he was pulled from his truck and severely beaten by a group of individuals. The unrest highlighted long-standing racial tensions and socio-economic disparities in Los Angeles.

In the aftermath of the riots, federal charges were brought against the officers involved in the beating of Rodney King. In 1993, two of the officers were found guilty of violating King's civil rights, while the other two were acquitted.

Rodney King became a symbol of police misconduct and the need for reform in law enforcement. The incident and its aftermath contributed to increased scrutiny of police practices, discussions about racial profiling, and calls for reform in the criminal justice system. Rodney King's story became a powerful symbol of the ongoing struggle for civil rights and justice in the United States.

Aftermath of the riots.
Mick Taylor from Portland, USA, CC BY-SA 2.0 <https://creativecommons.org/licenses/by-sa/2.0>, via Wikimedia Commons; https://commons.wikimedia.org/wiki/File:LA_Riots_-_aftermath_(159598182).jpg

77. In 1994, Paula Jones, a former Arkansas state employee, filed a sexual harassment lawsuit against Bill Clinton, then the governor of Arkansas. Jones alleged that Clinton had made unwanted sexual advances toward her in 1991. Clinton denied the allegations, but the lawsuit led to a series of investigations that would eventually culminate in his impeachment by the House of Representatives.

In 1996, Kenneth Starr, an independent counsel appointed by the attorney general, was tasked with investigating the Whitewater controversy, a scandal involving Clinton's investment in a failed real estate venture in Arkansas. During his investigation, Starr uncovered evidence of a sexual relationship between Clinton and

White House intern Monica Lewinsky. In 1998, Starr began investigating whether Clinton had committed perjury by denying the relationship with Lewinsky under oath. Clinton also testified before a grand jury about the Lewinsky matter and was questioned about his efforts to have Lewinsky deny the relationship.

In December 1998, the House of Representatives impeached Clinton on charges of perjury and obstruction of justice. The perjury charge related to his testimony about the Lewinsky affair, while the obstruction of justice charge arose from his attempts to influence Lewinsky's testimony and conceal evidence. Clinton's trial in the Senate began in January 1999.

After weeks of testimony and debate, the Senate acquitted Clinton on both charges. He remained in office and completed his second term as president. While the Senate ultimately acquitted him, the impeachment process left a lasting stain on his legacy and further polarized the American political landscape.

78. In August 1992, Randy Weaver, his wife Vicki, and their children were living on Ruby Ridge, a remote mountainous area in northern Idaho. The Weavers held anti-government and White supremacist views. Randy became a target of investigation by the Bureau of Alcohol, Tobacco, and Firearms (ATF) for selling illegal firearms.

The situation escalated on August 21ˢᵗ, 1992, when federal agents attempted to arrest Randy Weaver for his firearms violations. The Weavers resisted arrest, and a shootout ensued. During the exchange of gunfire, Deputy US Marshal William Degan and Weaver's teenage son, Samuel, were killed.

The FBI became involved, and a standoff developed. The standoff lasted eleven days, during which negotiations between the Weavers and federal authorities took place. The situation further escalated when FBI sniper Lon Horiuchi shot and killed Vicki Weaver while she was inside the family's cabin.

The Ruby Ridge standoff drew widespread attention and criticism, with concerns raised about the use of force by federal agents and questions about the tactics employed during the standoff. The incident also fueled anti-government sentiments and became a rallying point for various militia and extremist groups.

The subsequent trials of Randy Weaver and Kevin Harris (a family friend involved in the shootout) ended with Weaver acquitted of most charges and Harris acquitted of all charges except for one count of aiding and abetting the voluntary manslaughter of a federal officer.

The Ruby Ridge standoff had a lasting impact on public perception of government actions and the use of force, contributing to debates about the appropriate role of law enforcement in dealing with individuals holding anti-government views. It remains a significant and controversial chapter in the history of law enforcement and the interactions between the government and citizens.

79. On April 19th, 1995, the Alfred P. Murrah Federal Building in Oklahoma City burst into a monstrous plume of dust and debris. Timothy McVeigh, a veteran consumed by a toxic mix of anti-government anger and extremist beliefs, chose that building as his target, aiming to strike a blow against what he saw as a tyrannical state.

Disillusioned with the military after Waco and Ruby Ridge, McVeigh embraced radical anti-government ideologies and was fueled by conspiracy theories and a deep distrust of authority. He found like-minded individuals in the fringes of the militia movement, where his simmering rage found validation and twisted purpose.

Driven by this concoction of anger and warped ideals, McVeigh planned his act with chilling precision. A Ryder truck packed with fertilizer and fuel became his weapon, the Murrah building, housing a daycare center and government offices, his chosen battlefield. On that fateful morning, he detonated the bomb, shattering lives and the tranquility of Oklahoma City.

Baylee Almon was just one year old at the time of the bombing. She was in the second-floor daycare center of the Murrah Federal Building when the explosion occurred. The blast caused a portion of the building to collapse, including the daycare area.

In the aftermath of the bombing, a powerful and heart-wrenching photograph was captured by Charles H. Porter IV, a photojournalist who happened to be at the scene. The photograph showed Oklahoma City firefighter Chris Fields holding Baylee Almon, who was covered in dust and debris, as he carried her to safety. Baylee was limp, and her tiny body was a stark contrast to the strength and determination shown by the firefighter.

Tragically, Baylee Almon did not survive the bombing and was one of the 168 people who lost their lives that day. She had just celebrated her first birthday the day before the explosion. The image of her rescue became an iconic symbol of the tragedy and the heroism displayed by first responders and ordinary citizens who rushed to help in the explosion's aftermath.

80. On July 27th, 1996, during the Centennial Olympic Games in Atlanta, a bomb exploded in Centennial Olympic Park, a popular gathering place for spectators and athletes. The explosion occurred in the early morning hours during a concert attended by thousands of people. The blast resulted in two fatalities and injured over one hundred people, some of them critically.

The immediate response to the bombing was characterized by the heroism of first responders, medical personnel, and volunteers who provided assistance to the injured. Security guard Richard Jewell discovered the suspicious backpack containing the bomb before it exploded. His quick thinking and evacuation efforts likely saved many lives.

Initially, Richard Jewell was hailed as a hero for his actions, but he later became a suspect in the investigation due to a profiling analysis conducted by the FBI. His life was profoundly impacted by the media frenzy and suspicion surrounding him.

In 1997, Eric Robert Rudolph, a domestic terrorist, was arrested and subsequently pleaded guilty to the Centennial Olympic Park bombing, as well as other bombings. He was motivated by anti-abortion and anti-gay beliefs.

The bombing at the 1996 Summer Olympics underscored the need for enhanced security measures at major sporting events and public gatherings. Richard Jewell, who was wrongly accused in the initial stages of the investigation, later cleared his name, but the experience profoundly affected his life. He became an advocate for civil liberties and privacy rights.

The Centennial Olympic Park bombing was a tragic event that marred the 1996 Summer Olympics but also highlighted the resilience and heroism of those who responded to the crisis. It remains an important chapter in the history of both the Olympic Games and domestic terrorism in the United States.

Section 9 – A Defining Era: Transformative Events in American History from 2001 to 2021

In the years spanning from 2001 to 2021, America experienced a series of transformative events. The devastating 9/11 terrorist attacks reshaped the nation's foreign policy, leading to the War on Terror and military interventions in Afghanistan and Iraq. The financial crisis of 2008 provoked economic turmoil. The rise of social media also left a lasting impact on American society.

In this section, discover some interesting stories from America's not-so-distant past.

81. On September 11ᵗʰ, 2001, nineteen militants associated with the Islamic extremist group al-Qaeda hijacked four commercial airplanes and carried out suicide attacks against targets in the United States.

   The hijackers, most of whom were citizens of Saudi Arabia, boarded the planes armed with box cutters and knives. Once airborne, they took control of the cockpits and diverted the planes from their original destinations. At 8:46 a.m., American Airlines Flight 11 crashed into the north tower of the World Trade Center, followed by United Airlines Flight 175 at 9:03

a.m., which struck the south tower. Both towers collapsed within two hours, destroying surrounding buildings and damaging others.

At 9:37 a.m., American Airlines Flight 77 crashed into the western side of the Pentagon, causing a partial collapse of the building. Passengers and crew members aboard United Airlines Flight 93, which was headed for Washington, DC, fought back against the hijackers and regained control of the plane. The plane crashed in a field near Shanksville, Pennsylvania, at 10:03 a.m., killing all forty-four people on board.

Nearly three thousand people were killed in the attacks, which triggered major US initiatives to combat terrorism and defined the presidency of George W. Bush. The Bush administration argued that the threat of terrorism required the use of enhanced interrogation techniques, which critics labeled as torture. The administration also expanded domestic and international surveillance programs, raising concerns about privacy rights.

The 9/11 attacks were the deadliest terrorist attack in human history and had a profound impact on the United States and the world. The attacks led to the launch of the War on Terror, which included the invasion of Afghanistan and the overthrow of the Taliban government. The attacks also led to increased security measures at airports and other public places worldwide.

The explosion after the plane hit the South Tower.
https://commons.wikimedia.org/wiki/File:Explosion_following_the_plane_impact_into_the_South_Tower_(WTC_2)_-_B6019~11.jpg

82. In response to 9/11, the United States began military operations in Afghanistan, marking the beginning of the War on Terror. The United States' involvement in Afghanistan began on October 7th, 2001, with the launch of Operation Enduring Freedom, a military operation aimed at dismantling the al-Qaeda terrorist network and overthrowing the Taliban regime that had harbored them. The US-led coalition quickly achieved its initial objectives, removing the Taliban from power and establishing a new Afghan government. However, the US and its allies remained bogged down in Afghanistan for nearly two decades, facing a persistent insurgency and struggling to stabilize the country.

The US military went to other places as well. For years, intelligence agencies and special operations units worked to locate and apprehend Osama bin Laden, who had been evading capture since the attacks on September 11th, 2001. The search involved complex intelligence gathering, surveillance, and collaboration among various agencies.

The breakthrough in locating bin Laden came through years of tireless efforts and intelligence work. The Central Intelligence Agency (CIA) gradually pieced together information about a compound in Abbottabad, Pakistan, where they suspected bin Laden might be hiding. The compound, situated in a residential area near a military academy, raised suspicions due to its high walls, limited access, and lack of communication with the outside world.

In May 2011, President Barack Obama authorized a covert operation to raid the compound. On May 2nd, US Navy SEAL Team Six conducted a daring nighttime raid, penetrating Pakistani airspace without prior notification. The SEALs engaged in a firefight with those inside the compound, resulting in the death of Osama bin Laden.

The successful operation was a significant moment in the War on Terror, marking the end of a nearly decade-long hunt for the mastermind of the 9/11 attacks. The news of bin Laden's death was met with widespread relief and a sense of closure for many who had lost loved ones in the 2001 attacks.

The story of the hunt for Osama bin Laden and the operation that led to his death is a testament to the perseverance of intelligence and military professionals in pursuing justice and responding to acts of terrorism. The operation showcased the capabilities of special forces and highlighted the complex nature of counterterrorism efforts in the modern era.

83. The Iraq War, also known as *Operation Iraqi Freedom*, was a conflict that began in 2003 when a US-led coalition invaded Iraq to remove President Saddam Hussein from power. The war was primarily driven by concerns about Iraq's alleged possession of weapons of mass destruction (WMDs) and its links to terrorism. After Saddam Hussein's regime was toppled, Iraq faced a prolonged period of insurgency and instability, ultimately leading to the withdrawal of US troops in 2011.

During the Iraq War, an extraordinary act of bravery involved Private First Class Ross McGinnis, a US Army soldier. On December 4th, 2006, in Baghdad, Iraq, McGinnis was manning the machine gun turret of a Humvee while on patrol with his fellow soldiers. As the patrol moved through a crowded marketplace, an insurgent on a nearby rooftop threw a hand grenade into their Humvee.

McGinnis had a split-second decision to make. He could have jumped out of the turret to save himself, but instead, he selflessly sacrificed his life to protect his fellow soldiers. With incredible courage, McGinnis shouted a warning to his comrades and then used his own body to cover the live grenade, absorbing the full force of the explosion. His heroic actions saved the lives of four other soldiers in the vehicle, who survived the blast with only minor injuries.

Private First Class Ross McGinnis posthumously received the Medal of Honor, the highest military decoration in the United States, for his extraordinary bravery and sacrifice. His story serves as a powerful reminder of the selflessness and valor displayed by many individuals in the face of danger during times of conflict.

84. In September 2008, the global financial crisis peaked with Lehman Brothers' bankruptcy, causing widespread economic turmoil, job losses, and a severe recession in the United States

and much of Europe.

Lehman Brothers was a venerable Wall Street investment bank with a history dating back to the mid-19th century. However, by 2008, it found itself heavily exposed to the subprime mortgage market, which was in the midst of a significant downturn. The bank had invested heavily in mortgage-backed securities and faced mounting losses as the housing market declined. As Lehman Brothers faced severe financial distress in September 2008, the US government was reluctant to provide a bailout, unlike the interventions that had occurred with other financial institutions.

On September 15th, 2008, Lehman Brothers filed for Chapter 11 bankruptcy, marking one of the largest bankruptcies in US history. The collapse of Lehman Brothers had profound and far-reaching consequences. The interconnectedness of financial institutions meant that Lehman's bankruptcy had a domino effect, spreading fear and uncertainty throughout the financial system. The crisis prompted unprecedented government interventions, including the Troubled Asset Relief Program (TARP) in the United States, aimed to stabilize the financial sector.

The events of 2008 ultimately led to a severe economic recession with global repercussions, impacting individuals, businesses, and economies around the world. Lehman Brothers' downfall became a symbol of the excesses and risks within the financial industry, and the crisis highlighted the need for regulatory reforms to prevent a similar meltdown in the future. The 2008 financial crisis remains a significant chapter in economic history, influencing financial regulations and shaping perceptions of risk and responsibility in the financial sector.

85. On January 15th, 2009, US Airways Flight 1549, an Airbus A320, struck a flock of Canada geese shortly after takeoff from New York City's LaGuardia Airport. Both engines lost power, and Captain Chesley "Sully" Sullenberger and First Officer Jeffrey Skiles faced a dire situation.

With no engine power and limited options, Captain Sullenberger made the quick and daring decision to perform an emergency water landing in the frigid waters of the Hudson

River. Remarkably, all 155 passengers and crew on board survived the emergency landing and were able to evacuate the aircraft onto the wings and into nearby rescue boats.

Captain Sullenberger and First Officer Skiles were hailed as heroes for their cool-headed and skillful response to the crisis. Their experience and training played a critical role in the safe outcome.

The incident became a global media sensation, with the rescue efforts and interviews with passengers and crew members capturing the public's attention. The National Transportation Safety Board (NTSB) conducted an investigation, which confirmed the bird strike as the cause of the engine failure.

Both Captain Sullenberger and First Officer Skiles received numerous awards and recognition for their actions. The "Miracle on the Hudson" is a captivating and heartwarming story of heroism and quick thinking in the face of a life-threatening emergency. It demonstrated the importance of well-trained and experienced flight crews and showcased the potential for positive outcomes even in the most challenging situations.

The evacuation of the plane after landing in the Hudson River.

86. Jim Obergefell and John Arthur were a same-sex couple from Cincinnati, Ohio, who had been together for over two decades.

However, their relationship faced significant legal and societal challenges due to the lack of marriage equality in Ohio at the time. John was terminally ill with ALS (amyotrophic lateral sclerosis), and the couple's greatest wish was to have their marriage legally recognized before John's health deteriorated further.

In 2013, with the help of friends and family, Jim and John chartered a medical plane and flew to Maryland, where same-sex marriage was legal. They were married on the tarmac of Baltimore-Washington International Airport while John was lying on a gurney inside the plane.

After their wedding, Jim Obergefell and John Arthur filed a lawsuit challenging Ohio's refusal to recognize their marriage on John's death certificate. This case was consolidated with similar cases from other states and became known as *Obergefell v. Hodges*.

John Arthur died in 2013, but that didn't stop Obergefell; in fact, he became even more determined to see same-sex marriage be legalized.

On June 26th, 2015, the US Supreme Court issued a historic ruling in favor of marriage equality, declaring that same-sex marriage was a constitutional right nationwide. The decision meant that Jim Obergefell's marriage to John Arthur was legally recognized, allowing him to be listed as the surviving spouse on John's death certificate.

Jim Obergefell's personal journey to ensure that his marriage was recognized, even in the face of tragedy, became a powerful symbol of the fight for marriage equality in the United States. His dedication to love, justice, and civil rights played a significant role in the Supreme Court's landmark decision in *Obergefell v. Hodges*.

87. The Great Recession of 2008, triggered by the financial crisis, cast a long shadow on American society. Beyond the economic hardship, it severely affected public trust in key institutions, particularly banks and government agencies.

At its core, Occupy Wall Street wasn't simply a protest against the immediate economic crisis; it was a reaction to a perceived wider systemic injustice. Average Americans struggling with job losses, foreclosures, and dwindling savings witnessed a financial elite who were seemingly unscathed, their wealth protected by bailouts and regulations that appeared skewed in their favor. The image of Wall Street profiting from the wreckage while Main Street bore the brunt of the pain fueled a potent combination of anger and resentment.

Occupy Wall Street, with its diverse mix of participants, became a platform for expressing this collective disillusionment. The iconic "We are the 99%" slogan resonated deeply, uniting individuals under a shared sense of being wronged by a system that favored the privileged. Their encampments, such as the one at Zuccotti Park in New York City, became physical shelters and symbolic displays of dissent, challenging the power dynamics of the financial system and demanding greater accountability.

Many of the protesters showed a keen knowledge of history. During the 1929 stock market crash, several stockbrokers were said to have jumped from office windows on Wall Street since their entire fortune had been destroyed in just one or two days. Outside many of the large brokerage houses in 2008, some protesters held large signs saying "JUMP!" showing the anger many felt for the greed, mismanagement, and lack of government oversight that caused the financial crisis.

While Occupy Wall Street didn't directly alter the financial landscape, its impact extended beyond the immediate protests. It sparked important conversations about income inequality, corporate accountability, and the need for financial reform. It injected a dose of skepticism into public discourse, forcing institutions to acknowledge and address the concerns of ordinary citizens. Moreover, it demonstrated the power of collective action, proving that even a disparate group of individuals bound by shared frustration could raise their voices and make their concerns heard.

88. The emergence of social media gained significant traction in the 2000s, with platforms like Facebook and Twitter becoming increasingly popular. Social media revolutionized communication, information sharing, activism, and how people connect and interact globally.

But how did it start? Facebook gets the credit for making social media popular and accessible. Mark Zuckerberg and his college roommates Andrew McCollum, Eduardo Saverin, Chris Hughes, and Dustin Moskovitz launched Facebook from their dormitory at Harvard University in February 2004. Originally called "The Facebook," the platform was initially created as a way for Harvard students to connect with each other online. The site quickly gained popularity within the Harvard community, and expansion to other universities and colleges followed.

The turning point for Facebook's rapid expansion came in September 2006 when it opened its doors to the general public, allowing anyone with a valid email address to join. This move marked a significant departure from its earlier exclusivity to college students. The decision to open up the platform was driven by the desire to reach a broader audience and increase user engagement.

As Facebook continued to grow, it introduced new features, such as the news feed in 2006 and the like button in 2009, further enhancing the user experience. The platform's user base expanded globally, and by 2012, Facebook had reached one billion active users.

Facebook's success has had a profound impact on the way people communicate, share information, and connect online. It has also played a role in shaping the broader landscape of social media, influencing the development of other platforms, and contributing to the rise of a social media-centric culture in the 21st century.

89. In December 2019, President Trump signed the National Defense Authorization Act (NDAA) into law for the fiscal year of 2020. While the NDAA is a routine piece of legislation that funds the US military, this particular signing had a unique aspect that drew attention.

The John S. McCain National Defense Authorization Act for fiscal year 2019 included a provision requiring the US Navy to name a warship after Senator John McCain, who had served as a naval aviator during the Vietnam War. Senator McCain was known for his distinguished military service and later as a prominent politician.

During the signing ceremony for the NDAA in December 2019, President Trump did not mention Senator McCain by name nor acknowledge the ship naming provision. However, the story garnered attention when it was reported that a Navy destroyer, the USS *John S. McCain*, had been stationed in Japan, and a tarp had been placed over the ship's name to obscure it during President Trump's visit to a US Navy base in Yokosuka, Japan.

The incident sparked a debate about whether the tarp was placed intentionally to avoid mentioning Senator McCain's name in the president's presence or if it was for routine maintenance reasons. President Trump later tweeted that he was unaware of the tarp and had not requested it.

The tarp incident became a topic of discussion and scrutiny, reflecting the complex relationship between President Trump and Senator McCain, who had been a vocal critic of the president's policies and leadership style. It also highlighted the broader conversations around the intersection of politics, the military, and the recognition of public figures.

90. The United States maintained a military presence in Afghanistan from 2001 to 2021. Its presence in the country began after the 9/11 attacks. The mission initially aimed to dismantle al-Qaeda and remove the Taliban regime from power.

In February 2020, the Trump administration reached an agreement with the Taliban, setting a timeline for the withdrawal of US and NATO forces in exchange for Taliban commitments, including not harboring terrorists. In April 2021, President Joe Biden announced that the US would complete its withdrawal by August 31ˢ, 2021, ending nearly two decades of military involvement. The decision faced both support and criticism.

As the US withdrawal accelerated in 2021, the Taliban made rapid territorial gains. By August, they captured Kabul, leading to the collapse of the Afghan government.

The US and its allies initiated an emergency evacuation operation from Kabul airport to evacuate US citizens, Afghan allies, and vulnerable populations. The evacuation faced challenges due to the security situation and the sheer number of people needing assistance.

The US completed its military withdrawal by August 31st, 2021, marking the end of its combat mission in Afghanistan. The situation raised concerns about the fate of Afghan women, girls, and minorities under Taliban rule, as well as potential humanitarian crises.

Despite the military withdrawal, diplomatic efforts continued to address Afghanistan's future, including negotiations and international discussions. The withdrawal from Afghanistan was a complex and controversial process with significant implications for US foreign policy, regional stability, and the Afghan people. It marked the end of a lengthy military engagement and raised questions about the future of Afghanistan and the fight against terrorism in the region.

Section 10 – American Pop Culture: A World of Entertainment

Today, people are obsessed with celebrities, TV shows, movies, sports, and video games. That is not surprising. People have been invested in the lives of famous people, sports games, and media for millennia.

In this section, we will take a look at some interesting stories about American celebrities and pop culture.

91. In the early 20th century, during the height of the silent film era, one of the most iconic and enduring cinematic characters was created - Charlie Chaplin's "Tramp." The character was known for his distinctive appearance, featuring a bowler hat, a toothbrush mustache, a cane, and oversized shoes.

In 1914, when Chaplin was working at Keystone Studios, he was tasked with creating a new character for his next film. He quickly put together the Tramp's signature look using wardrobe items from the studio's costume department with just a few minutes to spare before shooting. Chaplin's Tramp character made its debut in the film *Kid Auto Races at Venice* (1914), and it was an instant success with audiences. The character's universal appeal and relatability transcended language barriers, making Chaplin an international superstar.

Over the years, the Tramp appeared in numerous silent films, including classics like *The Kid* (1921), *City Lights* (1931), and *Modern Times* (1936). The character was a symbol of resilience and optimism in the face of adversity, reflecting the challenges and hopes of the Great Depression era.

Charlie Chaplin's creation of the Tramp character remains an enduring and iconic contribution to the history of cinema. The character's influence can still be seen in popular culture today, and it serves as a testament to the power of silent films to convey emotion and connect with audiences worldwide.

Charlie Chaplin as the Tramp.
https://en.wikipedia.org/wiki/File:Charlie_Chaplin.jpg

92. In the 1920s, Jack Dempsey, known as the "Manassa Mauler," was one of the world's most celebrated and feared boxers. His famous bout against Luis Ángel Firpo on September 14th, 1923, became a historic moment in boxing history.

The fight took place at the Polo Grounds in New York City. Dempsey was the reigning World Heavyweight Champion, while Firpo was a hard-hitting Argentine heavyweight contender. What made this fight particularly memorable was the incredible first round.

The first round of the fight was nothing short of chaotic and exhilarating. Firpo, known for his aggressive style, unleashed a series of powerful punches that had Dempsey on the ropes. At one point in the round, Firpo landed a massive right hand that sent Dempsey crashing through the ropes and out of the ring. Dempsey's head narrowly missed hitting a typewriter on press row.

Dempsey's trainer, Jack Kearns, and the fight's referee, Johnny Gallagher, helped him back into the ring. According to the rules at the time, Dempsey had twenty seconds to return to the ring after being knocked out. He made it back just in time.

Despite the dramatic knockdown, Dempsey eventually regained his composure and fought back. He knocked Firpo down multiple times during the second round, and the fight was finally stopped, with Dempsey declared the winner.

Jack Dempsey's victory in his fight against Firpo was a testament to his resilience and punching power. It remains one of the most iconic moments in boxing history, showcasing the unpredictability and drama of the sport. The fight solidified Dempsey's status as a legendary figure in the world of boxing.

93. Bob Hope was one of the most iconic and beloved entertainers of the 20th century, known for his career in vaudeville, radio, film, and television. He became especially renowned for his decades-long commitment to entertaining American military personnel serving overseas.

Bob Hope's involvement with the USO (United Service Organizations) began during World War II when he performed his first show for servicemen and women in 1941. Throughout his career, he went on to entertain troops during World War II, the Korean War, the Vietnam War, and other conflicts. Hope's USO tours were extensive and covered various war zones and military bases worldwide. He traveled to places in the Pacific, Europe, the Middle East, and Southeast Asia, bringing laughter and a touch of home to American troops stationed far from their families.

Bob Hope's performances were more than just entertainment; they were a source of comfort and morale-boosting for servicemen and women in challenging and often dangerous circumstances. His shows provided a brief respite from the rigors of military life.

In addition to his performances, Bob Hope and his wife, Dolores, worked tirelessly to support military causes and raise funds for veterans. They were dedicated advocates for veterans' rights and welfare.

Bob Hope's dedication to the USO and the troops left a lasting legacy. He made his last USO tour in 1991, at the age of eighty-eight, making him one of the longest-serving supporters of the organization. The Bob Hope Airport in Burbank, California, was named in his honor, and he received numerous awards and recognitions for his contributions to the military and entertainment.

Bob Hope's commitment to bringing joy and laughter to the men and women serving in the armed forces exemplifies the power of entertainment to uplift spirits during challenging times. His USO tours remain a shining example of the positive impact that celebrities and entertainers can have on the lives of military personnel and their families.

94. In 1958, at the height of his music career, Elvis Presley received his draft notice to serve in the United States Army. Despite his fame and success, he didn't seek special treatment and chose to fulfill his military obligations like any other draftee.

Elvis joined the US Army on March 24th, 1958, and completed basic training at Fort Hood, Texas. During training, he endured the rigors of military life, including marching drills, physical fitness training, and marksmanship. Elvis's service didn't go unnoticed by the media and the public. His military service became major news stories, and it was widely reported that he had cut his famous sideburns and received a regulation military haircut.

While stationed in Germany from 1958 to 1960, Elvis served as a member of the 3rd Armored Division and continued to perform music during his off-duty hours. He also met his future wife, Priscilla Beaulieu, who lived in Germany at the time.

Despite his celebrity status, Elvis was treated like any other soldier and not given special privileges. He was often seen socializing with fellow soldiers and participating in military activities.

In 1960, after completing his two-year service, Elvis received an honorable discharge from the Army. He returned to his music career and went on to achieve even greater success in the entertainment industry. Elvis's military service is remembered not only for his willingness to serve his country but also for its impact on his personal life and career. It demonstrated his commitment to fulfilling his citizen duties and ability to adapt to different circumstances.

95. In the early 1950s, Walt Disney had a vision of creating a groundbreaking amusement park that would revolutionize the world of entertainment. He envisioned a place where both children and adults could enjoy attractions and entertainment and be able to immerse themselves in the magic of storytelling.

Walt's dream of a theme park was met with skepticism from many investors and industry experts. They believed amusement parks were dirty, chaotic, and unsuitable for families. Undeterred, Walt Disney was determined to turn his dream into a reality. He embarked on a mission to secure financing for his ambitious project.

Walt Disney faced numerous rejections from banks and potential investors. Many dismissed his idea as too risky. This period of his life became known as "Walt's Folly." However, Walt Disney's determination paid off when he successfully convinced ABC, the television network, to partner with him. In exchange for providing ABC with a weekly television show, Walt received financial support for Disneyland.

On July 17th, 1955, Disneyland opened its doors in Anaheim, California. Although it faced a rough opening day (known as "Black Sunday"), the park became a smash hit. The park featured various themed lands, including Adventureland, Fantasyland, and Tomorrowland, along with iconic attractions like Sleeping Beauty's Castle and the Jungle Cruise.

Disneyland became the prototype for future theme parks worldwide and solidified Walt Disney's reputation as an entertainment visionary. Today, Disneyland has expanded into a global brand, with multiple parks and resorts in different countries, each offering its own unique attractions and experiences.

96. In the late 1950s, Ruth Handler, co-founder of the toy company Mattel, noticed that her daughter, Barbara, often played with paper dolls and gave them adult roles. Handler envisioned creating a three-dimensional adult-like doll that could serve as a role model for young girls.

Inspired by a German doll called Bild Lilli, Handler and her husband Elliot set out to create a doll that was both fashionable and adult in appearance. They named the doll "Barbie" after their daughter.

In 1959, Mattel introduced the Barbie doll at the American International Toy Fair in New York City. The doll's official full name was Barbie Millicent Roberts, and she was marketed as a teenage fashion model.

Barbie quickly became a sensation. Her first outfits included a black-and-white striped swimsuit, sunglasses, and high heels, reflecting the fashion trends of the time. Over the years, Barbie has undergone numerous transformations and taken on various careers, fashion styles, and interests. She became a doctor, astronaut, teacher, athlete, and more, reflecting evolving societal roles for women.

Barbie's success extended beyond the toy industry. She became a cultural icon and inspired countless collectors, artists, and even fashion designers. Barbie dolls have been featured in various forms of media, including movies, TV shows, and books.

Despite occasional controversies related to body image and diversity, Barbie remains one of the world's most recognizable and enduring toy brands. In recent years, efforts have been made to diversify the Barbie line by introducing dolls of different ethnicities, body types, and careers.

The invention of the Barbie doll and its enduring impact on American pop culture is a fascinating story that highlights the influence of toys and fashion on society and the evolving representation of women in media and playtime. A movie about Barbie was made in 2023; it was a hit – a record-breaking box office success earning over $1.4 billion worldwide.

97. In the 1960s, during the height of the Vietnam War, Muhammad Ali, then known as Cassius Clay, became not only a boxing champion but also a prominent figure in the civil rights and anti-war movements.

In 1966, Ali received a notice for the military draft, which required him to serve in the US Army and potentially be deployed to Vietnam. At the time, Ali was the reigning World Heavyweight Champion. However, Ali refused to comply with the draft, citing his religious beliefs as a member of the Nation of Islam and his opposition to the war in Vietnam. He famously declared, "I ain't got no quarrel with them Viet Cong."

Ali's refusal to be drafted into the military led to a legal battle and significant controversy. During his prime years, he was stripped of his boxing titles and banned from the sport. Despite facing imprisonment and the loss of his boxing career, Ali stood firm in his convictions. He continued to speak out against the war and racial injustice in America.

In 1971, the US Supreme Court unanimously overturned Ali's conviction for draft evasion, citing that his beliefs as a conscientious objector were sincere and protected by the First Amendment. Following his legal victory, Muhammad Ali returned to boxing. He staged an epic comeback, culminating in the legendary "Thrilla in Manila" against Joe Frazier, a brutal three-part brawl that tested both men's limits.

Then came the "Rumble in the Jungle" in 1974. A thirty-two-year-old Ali, past his prime, faced the seemingly unstoppable George Foreman in Zaire. In a spectacle watched by millions, Ali deployed his "rope-a-dope" strategy, letting Foreman tire himself out before unleashing a devastating knockout in the eighth round. He reclaimed his title, proving that even a fallen champion could rise again.

Muhammad Ali's refusal to be drafted and his principled stand against the Vietnam War is a testament to his courage, conviction, and willingness to sacrifice his career for his beliefs. His stance made him a symbol of resistance to the war and a powerful advocate for civil rights and social justice.

Muhammad Ali and Joe Frazier's promotional photo.

98. On February 9th, 1964, The Beatles made their historic debut on the American television program *The Ed Sullivan Show*. This appearance is often regarded as a pivotal moment in the British Invasion and the band's rise to international superstardom.

Approximately seventy-three million viewers, or over 34 percent of the American population at the time, tuned in to watch The Beatles perform live on *The Ed Sullivan Show*. It remains one of the most-watched television broadcasts in US history.

The Beatles performed a set that included "All My Loving," "Till There Was You," "She Loves You," "I Saw Her Standing There," and "I Want to Hold Your Hand." Their energetic performance and charismatic presence captivated the audience. The screams of teenage girls in the studio and the electrifying atmosphere during the performance were captured by the cameras, creating an indelible image of "Beatlemania."

Following their Ed Sullivan appearance, The Beatles embarked on a whirlwind tour of the United States, performing in major cities and receiving an overwhelmingly positive reception. Among the frenzied crowd was fourteen-year-old future Oscar-nominated actress Sigourney Weaver, who already harbored dreams of the stage. She remembers The Beatles as "explosions of mop hair and energy." Their arrival must have felt like an alien invasion, not one of spaceships, but one of catchy tunes and teenage rebellion.

Their music, style, and personalities resonated with American youth. The Beatles' success on *The Ed Sullivan Show* marked the beginning of a wave of British bands and artists, including The Rolling Stones, The Who, and The Kinks, who achieved tremendous success in the United States during the British Invasion. The cultural impact of the British Invasion extended beyond music, influencing fashion, art, and youth culture in the 1960s and beyond. It helped bridge the gap between the United States and the United Kingdom, fostering a fascination with British pop culture.

99. *Jaws*, directed by Steven Spielberg and released in 1975, is widely considered the first summer blockbuster and one of the greatest films in cinematic history. However, the making of the film was fraught with challenges and setbacks.

The film, based on Peter Benchley's novel of the same name, tells the story of a small coastal town terrorized by a great white shark. Spielberg, a relatively young and unproven director at the time, was hired to helm the project.

One of the primary challenges during production was the mechanical shark used for the film, nicknamed "Bruce" after Spielberg's lawyer. The shark, which was supposed to be the film's central antagonist, suffered numerous technical malfunctions and delays, often leaving the production team frustrated. The mechanical shark's problems forced Spielberg to adopt a more suspenseful approach by showing the shark sparingly and relying on the iconic John Williams score to build tension. This decision became a defining element of the film's success.

Shooting on the open ocean presented additional challenges. The crew faced unpredictable weather, seasickness, and difficulties in capturing underwater footage.

The film's budget and shooting schedule also ballooned, far exceeding initial estimates. The production was initially slated for a 55-day shoot but extended to 159 days.

Despite the numerous obstacles, Spielberg's determination and creativity, combined with the commitment of the cast and crew, paid off. *Jaws* was completed and released in the summer of 1975. The movie became a massive success upon its release, breaking box office records and earning critical acclaim. It was a cultural phenomenon that not only revitalized the career of its director but also profoundly impacted the film industry by ushering in the era of blockbuster films.

The film's success led to sequels, theme park attractions, and a lasting legacy in popular culture. It also demonstrated the power of suspense and storytelling over visual effects, proving that limitations can lead to creative innovation.

100. In the early 1980s, the video game industry was booming, with home consoles like the Atari 2600 and a flood of new games hitting the market. It seemed like everyone was getting into gaming, and arcades were thriving.

However, the industry's rapid growth led to oversaturation and quality control issues. Many video games released during this period were of poor quality and often rushed to market to capitalize on the gaming craze.

In 1983, the video game market in the United States suffered a significant crash. It began with a combination of factors. First, too many games were available, causing consumer confusion and leading to a lack of demand for new titles. Many games released during this time were subpar, leading to disappointment among players. Additionally, the cost of video games and consoles was relatively high, making them less accessible to the average consumer. Personal computers, like the Commodore 64 and the Apple II, began to offer more sophisticated gaming experiences, diverting attention from traditional consoles.

As a result of these factors, sales of video games and consoles plummeted. Major companies, including Atari, suffered huge financial losses. To combat the crisis, Atari attempted to dispose of unsold inventory of their game *E.T. the Extra-Terrestrial* by burying thousands of unsold cartridges in a landfill in Alamogordo, New Mexico, a story that later became the stuff of legend.

The crash led to the bankruptcy of several video game companies and the downsizing of others. It also profoundly impacted the industry's reputation and consumer trust. However, the crash ultimately paved the way for a fresh start and the emergence of the Nintendo Entertainment System (NES) in 1985. Nintendo's strict quality control, iconic games like *Super Mario Bros.*, and a "Seal of Quality" certification system helped revitalize the industry and rebuild consumer confidence.

101. As you can see, history is not just the big political events, wars, and conflicts. In the 2000s and in the 2010s, America had a shining example of excellence to be proud of: Michael Phelps. He is one of the greatest Olympic athletes of all time.

Michael Phelps's journey in the Olympic pool is a saga etched in shimmering gold. Across five games, from Athens 2004 to Rio 2016, he carved his name into aquatic history, rewriting record books and amassing a staggering collection of medals. As of this writing, he has the most Olympic medals, earning twenty-eight in total, twenty-three of which are gold.

His Olympic odyssey began with youthful promise at Athens, where he captured six medals, four of them gold. Beijing 2008 witnessed his triumphant ascension, where he snagged a mind-boggling eight gold medals, surpassing Mark Spitz's record of seven, a feat many deemed untouchable. London 2012 saw him maintain his dominance, adding four more golds and two silvers to his tally.

Phelps's dominance wasn't solely about the sheer number of medals; it was the spectrum of events he mastered. He swam butterfly, freestyle, backstroke, and medley, demonstrating versatility and endurance unmatched in Olympic history. The 200-meter butterfly, an event he claimed ownership of, became his personal pool of invincibility, where he remained undefeated for eight years and won three consecutive Olympic golds.

But Phelps's story transcends the glittering hardware. He battled personal demons outside the pool, grappling with depression and substance abuse. His 2016 comeback, after a brief retirement marked by controversy, was a testament to his resilience and unwavering passion for the sport. His final Olympic race, the men's 4x100-meter medley race in Rio, wasn't about adding another gold to his collection (although he did); it was a victory lap, a poignant farewell to a legend returning to the very pool where his journey began.

Conclusion

As we bring our journey through American history to a close, it becomes abundantly clear that this nation is a mosaic of seemingly disparate yet deeply interconnected narratives. From the humble beginnings of colonization to the untamed spirit of Manifest Destiny, from the crucible of the Civil War to the triumphs of the civil rights movement, each chapter represents a thread woven into the vibrant tapestry of American society. These stories serve as a reminder that this nation is not just a mere collection of dates, names, and events but also a living, breathing story of resilience, determination, and everlasting pursuit of freedom.

As we move forward, let us embrace past lessons and strive to amplify the voices that have long been silenced, ensuring that the arc of American history bends ever closer toward justice, equality, and unity.

If you enjoyed this book, a review on Amazon would be greatly appreciated because it would mean a lot to hear from you.

To leave a review:

1. Open your camera app.
2. Point your mobile device at the QR code.
3. The review page will appear in your web browser.

Thanks for your support!

Check out another book in the series

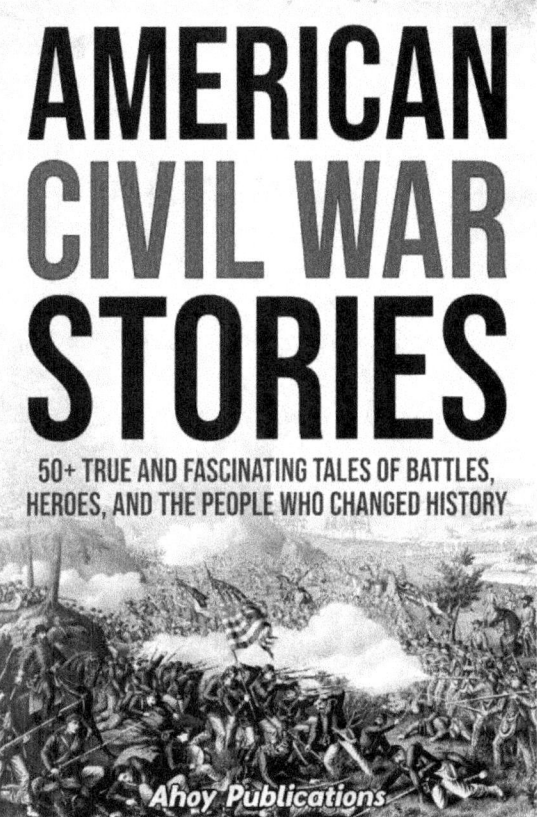

Bibliography

Allison, Robert. *The American Revolution: A Concise History.* Oxford UP, 2011.

Anderson, Fred. *The War That Made America: A Short History of the French and Indian War.* Penguin, 2006.

Bapat, Navin A. *Monsters to Destroy: Understanding the War on Terror.* Oxford UP, USA, 2019.

Bernstein, Carl, and Bob Woodward. *All the President's Men.* Simon & Schuster, 1974.

Brands, H. W. *Reagan: The Life.* Anchor, 2016.

Bullard, Sara. *Free at Last: A History of the Civil Rights Movement and Those Who Died in the Struggle.* Oxford UP, USA, 1994.

Burgan, Michael. *The Great Depression: An Interactive History Adventure.* Capstone, 2011.

Cashman, Sean D. *America in the Gilded Age: From the Death of Lincoln to the Rise of Theodore Roosevelt.* NYU P, 1993.

Cave, Alfred A. *The Pequot War.* 1996.

Charles River Charles River Editors. *The Election of 1828: The History of the Race Between Andrew Jackson and John Quincy Adams That Ended the Era of Good Feelings.* Createspace Independent Publishing Platform, 2018.

Chernow, Ron. *Washington: A Life.* Penguin UK, 2010.

Conti-Brown, Peter. *The Power and Independence of the Federal Reserve.* Princeton UP, 2017.

Cringely, Robert. *The Decline and Fall of IBM: End of an American Icon?* Nerdtv, LLC, 2014.

Detzer, David. *Allegiance: Fort Sumter, Charleston, and the Beginning of the Civil War.* Houghton Mifflin Harcourt, 2002.

DuBois, Ellen C. *Suffrage: Women's Long Battle for the Vote.* Simon & Schuster, 2021.

Fitzgerald, Brian. *The Korean War: America's Forgotten War.* Capstone, 2006.

Foer, Franklin. *The Last Politician: Inside Joe Biden's White House and the Struggle for America's Future.* Penguin, 2023.

Foner, Eric. *Reconstruction: America's Unfinished Revolution, 1863-1877.* HarperCollins, 2011.

Friedman, Jeffrey. *What Caused the Financial Crisis.* U of Pennsylvania P, 2011.

Gaddis, John L. *The Cold War: A New History.* Penguin, 2006.

Gitlin, Marty. *Brown v. Board of Education.* ABDO, 2007.

Glaser, Jason. *John Brown's Raid on Harpers Ferry.* Capstone, 2006.

Goodwin, Doris K. *Team of Rivals: The Political Genius of Abraham Lincoln.* Penguin UK, 2009.

Gordon, Michael R., and Bernard E. Trainor. *The Generals' War: The Inside Story of the First Gulf War.* Atlantic, 2006.

Gray, Derek. *NAACP in Washington, D.C.: From Jim Crow to Home Rule.* American Heritage, 2022.

Gray, Edward G., and Jane Kamensky. *The Oxford Handbook of the American Revolution.* Oxford UP, 2015.

Gunderson, Jessica. *The Triangle Shirtwaist Factory Fire.* Capstone, 2006.

Guttenberg, Fred, and Thomas Gabor. *American Carnage: Shattering the Myths That Fuel Gun Violence.* Mango Media, 2023.

Hankins, Barry. *The Second Great Awakening and the Transcendentalists.* Greenwood, 2004.

Harris, Duchess, and Bonnie Hinman. *The Freedmen's Bureau.* ABDO, 2019.

Haskew, Michael E. *Appomattox: The Last Days of Robert E. Lee's Army of Northern Virginia.* Zenith P, 2015.

Hinderaker, Eric. *Boston's Massacre.* Harvard UP, 2017.

Hinman, Bonnie. *The Massachusetts Bay Colony: The Puritans Arrive from England.* Mitchell Lane Publishers, 2010.

Hinton, KaaVonia. *To Preserve the Union: Causes and Effects of the Missouri Compromise.* Capstone, 2013.

Jr., Frank E., and Daniel B. Smith. *Jamestown Colony: A Political, Social, and Cultural History*. Bloomsbury Publishing USA, 2007.

Karnow, Stanley. *Vietnam: A History*. Penguin, 1997.

Leuchtenburg, William E. *Franklin D. Roosevelt and the New Deal: 1932-1940*. Harper Perennial, 2009.

McCullough, David. *The Path Between the Seas: The Creation of the Panama Canal, 1870-1914*. Simon & Schuster, 2001.

McCullough, David. *Truman*. Simon & Schuster, 2003.

McDonald, Allan J. *Truth, Lies, and O-Rings: Inside the Space Shuttle Challenger Disaster*. UP of Florida, 2012.

McMillen, Sally. *Seneca Falls and the Origins of the Women's Rights Movement*. Oxford UP, 2009.

McPherson, James M. *Battle Cry of Freedom: The Civil War Era*. Oxford UP, 2003.

Merry, Robert W. *A Country of Vast Designs: James K. Polk, the Mexican War and the Conquest of the American Continent*. Simon & Schuster, 2010.

Messerli, Jonathan. *Horace Mann: A Biography*. Knopf, 1972 [c1971], 1972.

Meyer, G. J. *The World Remade: America in World War I*. Bantam, 2018.

Michel, Lou, and Dan Herbeck. *American Terrorist: Timothy McVeigh & the Tragedy at Oklahoma City*. Harper, 2002.

Miller, Nathan. *New World Coming: The 1920s and the Making of Modern America*. Simon & Schuster, 2010.

Montgomery, Dennis. *1607: Jamestown and the New World*. Rowman & Littlefield Publishers, 2007.

Morris, Edmund. *The Rise of Theodore Roosevelt*. Modern Library, 2010.

Murray, Charles A., and Catherine B. Cox. *Apollo*. 2004.

Musicant, Ivan. *Empire by Default: The Spanish-American War and the Dawn of the American Century*. Owl Books, 2008.

Nelson, Michael, et al. *42: Inside the Presidency of Bill Clinton*. Cornell UP, 2016.

Otis, D. S. *The Dawes Act and the Allotment of Indian Lands*. U of Oklahoma P, 2014.

Painter, Nell I. *Standing at Armageddon: A Grassroots History of the Progressive Era*. W. W. Norton & Company, 2011.

Polmar, Norman, and John D. Gresham. *DEFCON-2: Standing on the Brink of Nuclear War During the Cuban Missile Crisis*. 2006.

Rhodes, Richard. *Arsenals of Folly: The Making of the Nuclear Arms Race*. Vintage, 2008.

Ross, John F. *Enduring Courage: Ace Pilot Eddie Rickenbacker and the Dawn of the Age of Speed.* Macmillan, 2014.

Sarotte, Mary E. *1989: The Struggle to Create Post-Cold War Europe - Updated Edition.* Princeton UP, 2014.

Saunt, Claudio. *Unworthy Republic: The Dispossession of Native Americans and the Road to Indian Territory.* W. W. Norton & Company, 2020.

Schermerhorn, Calvin. *Unrequited Toil: A History of United States Slavery.* Cambridge UP, 2018.

Schultz, Eric B., and Michael J. Tougias. *King Philip's War: The History and Legacy of America's Forgotten Conflict.* The Countryman P, 2000.

Sexton, Jay. *The Monroe Doctrine: Empire and Nation in Nineteenth-Century America.* Hill and Wang, 2011.

Steinhauer, Jason. *History, Disrupted: How Social Media and the World Wide Web Have Changed the Past.* Springer Nature, 2021.

Stewart, David O. *The Summer of 1787: The Men Who Invented the Constitution.* Simon & Schuster, 2008.

Stewart, James B. *Holy Warriors: The Abolitionists and American Slavery.* Macmillan, 1996.

Stick, David. *Roanoke Island: The Beginnings of English America.* UNC P Books, 2015.

Stowell, David O. *Streets, Railroads, and the Great Strike of 1877.* U of Chicago P, 1999.

Tuchman, Barbara W. *The Guns of August: The Outbreak of World War I; Barbara W. Tuchman's Great War Series.* Random House, 2009.

Wallace-Wells, David. *The Uninhabitable Earth: Life After Warming.* Crown, 2020.

Washburn, Wilcomb E. *The Governor and the Rebel: A History of Bacon's Rebellion in Virginia.* UNC P Books, 2018.

Weinberg, Gerhard L. *A World at Arms: A Global History of World War II.* Cambridge UP, 2005.

Whiting, Jim. *The Maryland Colony: Lord Baltimore.* Mitchell Lane Publishers, 2010.

Wood, Gordon S. *The Radicalism of the American Revolution.* Knopf, 1992.

Woodward, Bob. *Fear: Trump in the White House.* Simon & Schuster, 2018.

Wright, Lawrence. *The Looming Tower: Al-Qaeda and the Road to 9/11.* Vintage, 2018.

Yero, Judith L. *The Mayflower Compact.* National Geographic Books, 2006.

Zelizer, Julian. *The Presidency of Barack Obama: A First Historical Assessment.* Princeton UP, 2018.